Power Tools

Building Foundations: A Spirit Filled Children's Church Curriculum

Pastor Tamera Kraft
Revival Fire 4 Kids Resource

Includes:
Prayer Power
Worship Power
Holy Spirit Power

Mt Zion Ridge Press
http://mtzionridgepress.com
Managing Editors: Michelle L. Levigne and Tamera Lynn Kraft
Cover Art: Tamera Lynn Kraft

ISBN: 978-1-955838-06-1

Registration and Digital Files (Available for FREE with purchase of the curriculum): Digital files (jpeg graphics, video clips, other resources) are available to anyone who purchases and registers this curriculum at no additional cost. To register, click on this link http://eepurl.com/glsELH or type it in the address box on your browser and fill out the form. We never sell or give away any information we receive.

DVD: If you prefer a DVD of Jpeg images and video clips, you may purchase it at http://mtzionridgepress.com for an additional cost.

Power Tools is a 3 part curriculum which includes these sections that can be bought together in one manual or bought separately:

- Part 1 – Prayer Power (4 lessons on the power of prayer included in this manual)
- Part 2 – Worship Power (4 Lessons on the power of worshipping God)
- Part 3 – Holy Spirit Power (5 lessons on how the baptism and gifts of the Holy Spirit equip you with power)

Power Tools is available in PDF download and print. Each part of *Power Tools* is available separately in PDF download or print.

All Scripture in this curriculum is from the NIV (2011) Bible unless otherwise designated.

For questions about copyright issues or other matter concerning rights for this curriculum, contact revivalfire4kids@att.net.

Building Foundations Curriculum is a Revival Fire for Kids resource. For more information about Revival Fire for Kids, check out their website at http://revivalfire4kids.net

Materials included:

Prayer Power: 4 complete downloadable lessons including 8 object lessons, 8 skits, 8 games, 4 Bible Stories, 4 memory verse activities, graphics to be used in PowerPoint slides for 8 lessons, 4 small group discussions, and

optional lessons and activities. Lessons, graphics, videos, and Family Devotion Handouts will be available for immediate download.

Worship Power: 4 complete downloadable lessons including 8 object lessons, 8 skits, 8 games, 4 Bible Stories, 8 Worship Expression Lessons, 4 memory verse activities, graphics to be used in PowerPoint slides for 4 lessons, 4 small group discussions, and optional lessons and activities. Lessons, graphics, videos, and Family Devotion Handouts will be available for immediate download.

Holy Spirit Power: 5 complete downloadable lessons including 10 object lessons, 10 skits, 10 games, 5 Bible Stories, 5 memory verse activities, graphics to be used in PowerPoint slides for 5 lessons, 5 small group discussions or activities, and optional lessons and activities.

Lessons, graphics, videos, and Family Devotion Handouts will be available for immediate download upon registering this curriculum at this link: http://eepurl.com/glsELH.

Table of Contents

How To Use This Curriculum:

Scriptural Premise: God does not leave us powerless in our Christian journey. He gives us tools to empower us for everything He wants us to do. Among these power tools are prayer, worship, the baptism of the Holy Spirit, and the gifts of the Holy Spirit.

Decorations: Decorations and set design should reflect building construction with drills, saws, and power tools. If you have purchased *The Journey*, another *Building Foundations Curriculum*, you could use the decorations for *The Journey* and add power tools. You could also borrow power tools from someone and set up a power tools garage or store.

Another idea is to use a backdrop with the cover picture of *Power Tools or Power Tools* backdrop as templates for a backdrop. You can use any image included with this curriculum by projecting the image using a video projector onto a box or backdrop and drawing it. Use your creativity.

Italics: Italics are used for Scripture. They are also used in this curriculum for passages or speeches the teacher or worker may want to say in their own words. For skits, italics are only used to designate the person speaking.

Registration and Digital Files (Available for FREE with purchase of the curriculum): Digital files (jpeg graphics, video clips, other resources) are available to anyone who purchases and registers this curriculum at no additional cost. To register, click on this link http://eepurl.com/glsELH or type it in the address box on your browser and fill out the form. We never sell or give away any information we receive.

Welcome:

Welcome: Each lesson will welcome the children with an introduction to that day's message.

Prayer: It's important to start each lesson with prayer.

Rules: A list of 5 Ups are included in the graphics available after registration. Rehearse the rules every week.

Theme Song: Get the kids up and moving at the beginning of every lesson with a fun theme song. Theme song that will work with this curriculum are *There is Power* by Lincoln Brewster, *Rest on Us* by Maverick City Music, *Power (Acts 1:8 ESV)* by Seeds Family Worship, or *Waymaker* by Leeland.

Memory Verse: Every lesson has a memory verse. The verse will be included in a slide and will be illustrated in three ways. You can choose to use any of these illustrations to teach the verse, or you could use all three throughout your lesson.

Memory Verse Skit: A puppet or live skit with Doctor Word is included in each lesson to introduce the Memory Verse. The person doing the skit can dress as a doctor or in scrubs. If a doctor, nurse, or medical professional attends you church, it would be great to him for your skits and have him wear his work clothes. You can also use a doctor puppet for these skits if you have a puppet team.

Memory Verse Talk: This is a short talk explaining what the verse means to the children. Memorizing God's Word is important, but it's more important for your students to know what a verse means.

Memory Verse Activity: Children learn by seeing, reading, hearing, and doing. The memory verse activity is a simple tool to help students remember the verse.

Game Time: A Game Time slide is included with registration for this curriculum. It isn't necessary to include a game with every week's lesson, but if you do, you should have a fun game that relates to the lessons. Game Time is the place for that. You may also want to save the game for last so, if the adult service runs long, you can play games until the parents arrive to retrieve their children.

Video Clips: *Power Tools Countdown* and video clips for some lessons are included with *Holy Spirit Power* along with other downloadable files. A link to a Dropbox files with be sent to your email after you have registered your curriculum. *Building Foundations* doesn't provide video curriculum to teach the lessons. Instead, it provides short, fun video clips to help the children remember the lesson in a fun way. To register, click on this link http://eepurl.com/glsELH or type it in the address box on your browser and fill out the form.

Offering: Lessons include a short talk on why children should give in the offering. You can expand the fun by having an offering contest with the boys against the girls. You can use a scale with buckets or have two offering plates and count the money. Once a month or once a quarter, have a special reward for the winning team.

Praise & Worship: Each week, a time of praise and worship is included to ready the students' hearts to hear the Word of God. This curriculum does not provide music because every church has different musical needs.

Lesson of the Week:

Skit: Two skits about each week's lesson are included. One skit uses a doctor, Doctor Word, to introduce the memory verse for the day. Another skit uses a silly character named Tyler the Power Tool Guy or Gal. These skits require few props and only two people, the leader and another worker, making them easy for even small churches to use. Doctor Word skits can be used as puppet skits if you have a puppet ministry. Tyler the Power Tool Guy or Gal could also be used with puppets but may need some modification when props are involved.

Bible Story: Each week, a Bible story is included to go with the lesson.

Object Lessons: At least two object lessons illustrate the points of each week's lesson. Resources for the object lessons are not included.

Message: A short message ties up the lesson for the day and asks for a response from the students.

Optional Resources: Optional Resources are included in some lessons with object lessons and other interactive events as suggestions for additional teaching activities. The props for optional resources are not included but are easy to obtain.

Small Group Chat/Activity: Some children's ministries prefer to end each children's service with a small group chat, or they have a small group Bible study at some time during the week. Small group chat questions and activities are included for these purposes. Divide students into small groups of not more than six children. You can divide them by ages or include different ages together. Questions and instructions for activities are included to help the leader facilitate a chat with the students about the lesson. Small group sessions will help your students go home with practical applications for what they have learned.

Home Application: Each lesson will include a handout for the children to take home. Each handout will include this week's memory verse, a summary of the lesson, a Bible reading for each day, and a weekly family activity. This handout is available as a printable PDF download upon registration of this curriculum. This will be helpful guide for parents who have family devotions. To register, click on this link http://eepurl.com/glsELH or type it in the address box on your browser and fill out the form.

Registration and Digital Files (Available for FREE with purchase of the curriculum): Digital files (jpeg graphics, video clips, other resources) are available to anyone who purchases and registers this curriculum at no additional cost. To register, click on this link http://eepurl.com/glsELH or type it in the address box on your browser and fill out the form. We never sell or give away any information we receive.

Power Tools Part 1: Prayer Power Lessons

Power Tools 1: Prayer Power Lessons

5 Finger Prayer

Matthew 6:9-13 (NKJV) *Our Father in heaven, Hallowed be Your name. Your kingdom come. Your will be done On earth as it is in heaven. Give us this day our daily bread. And forgive us our debts, As we forgive our debtors. And do not lead us into temptation, But deliver us from the evil one. For Yours is the kingdom and the power and the glory forever. Amen.*

Don't Worry - Pray

Philippians 4:6 (ICB) *"Do not worry about anything. But pray and ask God for everything you need. And when you pray, always give thanks."*

FAITH Prayer

Matthew 17:20 … *If you have faith as small as a mustard seed, you can say to this mountain, 'Move from here to there,' and it will move. Nothing will be impossible for you.*

Powerful Prayer

James 5: 16 … *The prayer of a righteous person is powerful and effective.*

Lesson 1 – 5 Finger Prayer

Focus Point: Jesus taught us how to pray.

Goal: Students will learn the Lord's Prayer model to help them prayer.

Verse of the Day: **Matthew 6:9-13 (NKJV)** ... *Our Father in heaven, Hallowed be Your name.*

Your kingdom come. Your will be done On earth as it is in heaven.

Give us this day our daily bread. And forgive us our debts, As we forgive our debtors.

And do not lead us into temptation, But deliver us from the evil one.

For Yours is the kingdom and the power and the glory forever. Amen.

Supplies Needed:

- doctor puppet or doctor costume for skit
- portable toolbox with various tools
- Tyler the Power Tool Guy Skit: Tyler wears a portable toolbox or toolbelt with various tools and is dressed in blue jeans and a plaid shirt, etc.
- power screwdriver
- paper plate
- bread
- lunchmeat
- lettuce
- ketchup, mustard, and other sandwich elements
- cheese
- Marker board, chalk board, or blank wall
- scotch tape
- 1 set of strips of paper or poster board
- marker board
- poster
- rock
- rubber snake
- bread
- toy fish

Opening: *Power Tools Countdown* or *Power Tools* Slide (Available free with registration of this curriculum.)

Welcome: *Welcome to Power Tools. For the next few weeks, we will learn about one of the most powerful tools in a Christian's life, the power of prayer. Prayer is more than saying the right words. Prayer is talking the King of Kings and Lord of Lords. Prayer is talking to God.*

Prayer: Ask a child to pray over the service.

Rules: (use rules slide) Go over the 5 Ups Rules.

Go over the *5 Ups Rules*: 1. Sit up straight. 2. Listen up. 3. Hush up. 4. Don't get up and run around or go to the bathroom. 5. Worship Up! (stand up and participate during praise and worship)

Theme or Activity Songs: Choose one of two fast moving activity or theme songs that go with the curriculum.

Game Time: Telephone (use game time slide)

Supplies Needed: none

This is the traditional game of telephone. Whisper "Our Father in Heaven. Hallowed be Your Name," in the first student's ear. Have that student whisper into the next student's ear. Continue until it reaches the last student. Have that student announce what he heard.

When playing telephone, it's important to speak clearly and listen carefully. That's true in prayer too. God wants us to speak clearly to Him about everything in our hearts, and He also wants us to listen.

Memory Verse Skit: (use Prayer Power Lesson 1, slide A)

Supplies needed: doctor puppet or doctor costume for skit

Doctor Word: Hi kids. I'm Doctor Word. I'm called that because I'm a doctor and because I love the Word of God. As a doctor, I use a lot of tools. One of the most important tools I use is a stethoscope. A stethoscope is one of the most powerful tools a doctor has because it amplifies sound. I can use it to check my patient's heart, lungs, and even listen to their stomach.

That reminds me of one of the most important power tools we have as Christians – prayer. That's why it's important to learn how to pray. When Jesus' disciples asked Him how to pray, He gave them an example of how to pray. It's called the Lord's Prayer, and it is our memory verse for this week.

In Matthew 6:9-13, Jesus said, *"Our Father in heaven, Hallowed be Your name. Your kingdom come. Your will be done On earth as it is in heaven. Give us this day our daily bread. And forgive us our debts, As we forgive our debtors. And do not lead us into temptation, But deliver us from the evil one. For Yours is the kingdom and the power and the glory forever. Amen."*

Remember, tools don't work unless you use them, so let's decide to use our Prayer Power tool every day.

Offering:

Did you ever wonder why we pray over the offering before we take it? I did when I was younger. Then my teacher told me how we should pray over everything. Praying over the offering we give helps us to remember that God makes it more effective in the Kingdom of God. We should pray that God will use it for His glory. So, let's pray over the offering now.

Skit: Tyler the Power Tool Guy Doesn't Have the Tool He Needs

Supplies Needed: Tyler has a portable toolbox or toolbelt with various tools and is dressed in blue jeans and a plaid shirt, etc., power screwdriver. If you use a girl in the skit, have her dress the same and call her Tyler the Power Tool Gal.

(Tyler, the Power Tool Guy, comes into the room carrying an electric screwdriver. He plugs it in and starts revving it up.)

Leader: Excuse me, Sir. We're having children's church here, and you're interrupting.

Tyler the Power Tool Guy: (looks around like he just noticed everyone) Well, hello there. I'm as sorry as I can be for interrupting, but I have a work order to replace an outlet in this room.

Leader: Do you have to replace it now?

Tyler: I just do what they tell me. It will only take a moment. See, I have this power tool with different size bits. I just need to find the right one to unscrew the screws, and I'll be done in no time.

Leader: That is a nice screwdriver, but—

Tyler: Yes, it is. I got it at the Acme Power Tools Store. It has 6,000 different size bits, one for every kind of screw.

Leader: Don't you have to turn off the electric before you can change the outlet?

Tyler: Turn off the electric? Good idea. As soon as I find the right head for my screwdriver, I'll go do that.

Leader: Tyler, I'm going to have to insist you wait to change out the outlet. We're right in the middle of teaching these children. You can't turn off the electricity now.

Tyler: I'm powerful sorry, but this can't wait. As soon as I find the right bit, I'll have to turn off the power and change the outlet, but I'll be out of here in no time. (Starts looking through different bits. Distractedly asks question.) What are you teaching these kids?

Leader: I'm teaching them about spiritual power tools like prayer.

Tyler: Spiritual power tools. I don't have any of them. I thought I had every power tool there is. I'm going to have to go to Acme Power Tools Store and get me one of them.

Leader: You can't find prayer at a store. Prayer is talking to God. Today, we're teaching the children about the different components of prayer.

Tyler: Like different bits for a screwdriver?

Leader: Not exactly. With prayer, we have the ability to talk to God any time we want.

Tyler: Well, I'll get out of your hair as soon as I find the right bit for this screwdriver. I believe I need a Phillips Number Three. (rifles through screwdrivers) Oh no, 6,000 heads, and I don't have a Phillips Three. I need to go to Acme Power Tools Store and complain. (Packs up tools and leaves.)

Leader: Maybe Tyler, the Power Tool Guy, needs Prayer Power to help him find the right screwdriver head.

(Exits)

Verse of the Day: Matthew 6:9-13 (NKJV)

...Our Father in heaven, Hallowed be Your name.

Your kingdom come. Your will be done on earth as it is in heaven.

Give us this day our daily bread. And forgive us our debts, as we forgive our debtors.

And do not lead us into temptation, But deliver us from the evil one.

For Yours is the kingdom and the power and the glory forever. Amen.

Memory Verse Talk: Praise Sandwich (use Prayer Power Lesson 1, slide A)

Supplies needed: paper plate, bread, lunchmeat, lettuce, ketchup, mustard, and other sandwich elements, cheese

Did you ever wonder why people want you to memorize the Lord's prayer? After all, if prayer is just talking to God, why would we want to memorize a prayer. The importance of this prayer is not that we recite every word correctly. God doesn't want that kind of prayer. This prayer is a model for prayer. It helps us know how to pray. I'm going to illustrate this by making a praise sandwich.

First, we start with praising God. Place bread on the plate. *We'll use a slice of bread to show the praise.*

Then we let God know we want His will for our lives. This is one of the most important parts of prayer, so I'll use the lunchmeat to show God's will. Place a piece of lunch meat on the bread. *This is such an important part of the sandwich that I don't want to only use one slice.* Place two more slices of lunchmeat on the sandwich.

After that, we can start giving God our prayer requests. Everyone's prayer requests are different just as everyone likes different things on their sandwiches. Place each element on the sandwich as you talk about it. *Some people like lettuce. Others only want ketchup and mustard.*

The next part tops off the sandwich with something most people love – cheese. Place cheese on the sandwich. *When we pray, it's important to ask God to forgive us for anything we've done wrong and to ask God to help us forgive others. We don't only want God's forgiveness, though. We also want Him to help us do what's right and avoid what's evil. Just as cheese makes a sandwich better, this helps us live a better Christian life.*

This sandwich still needs something. Can you guess what it is? Have the children guess. If they don't guess bread right away, point to the bread to give them a hint. Place slice of bread on top.

A sandwich needs two slices of bread to make it easier to eat. And every prayer should start and end with praise. So, I guess you could say prayer is a praise sandwich.

Memory Verse Activity: Prayer Strips

Supplies needed: Marker board, chalk board, or blank wall; scotch tape; 1 set of strips of paper or poster board for each team with the following written on each sheet:

...Our Father in heaven, Hallowed be Your name.

Your kingdom come. Your will be done on earth as it is in heaven.

Give us this day our daily bread. And forgive us our debts, as we forgive our debtors.

And do not lead us into temptation, But deliver us from the evil one.

For Yours is the kingdom and the power and the glory forever. Amen.

Matthew 6:9-13 (NKJV)

Assign the children to teams. You can have up to six children on each team. When you say go, children from each team will arrange the lines of verse in order with the verse address at the end. They will tape the papers in order on the marker boards or walls. If you have a large group of students, you could have teams take turns doing this.

Bible Story: Jesus teaches His Disciples to Pray

(Matthew 6:5-14; Luke 11:1-4)

Supplies needed: marker board, poster, or projection device

If you could ask Jesus to teach you to do anything, what would you ask Him to teach you. If your students don't answer at first, make suggestions. Write down all the answers.

Jesus' disciples were always being taught by Him, but when they asked Jesus to teach them, what do you think they asked for? The disciples asked Jesus to teach them to pray. Prayer must be very important if that's the one thing the disciples wanted to learn. Jesus taught the disciples this prayer, not because he wanted them to memorize it and recite it every time they prayed. The prayer was an example of things they could pray for. Let's look over the prayer again and think about the things Jesus told the disciples they could pray for.

... Our Father in heaven, Hallowed be Your name. Hallowed means honored or praised. So, Jesus wants us to start our prayers by praising God, our Heavenly Father. That's a great way to start a prayer.

Your kingdom come. Your will be done on earth as it is in heaven. Jesus wants us to pray for God's will to be done on the Earth. For instance, when you pray for your friend to know Jesus, you're praying for God's will to be done because God wants everyone to be saved.

Give us this day our daily bread. That's when we pray for the things we need and want. God is interested in our wants and desires as well as the things we need.

And forgive us our debts, as we forgive our debtors. If you have done anything God is not pleased with, this is the time to ask for forgiveness, but it's also the time to forgive anyone who has done something wrong to you.

And do not lead us into temptation, But deliver us from the evil one. We can't resist doing bad things on our own, but we can pray and ask God to help us do what's right.

For Yours is the kingdom and the power and the glory forever. Amen. This shows we end the prayer by praising God. Amen means "so be it". It's a way to show we have faith that God will answer our prayers. Now let's praise God.

Praise and Worship: Choose a couple of fast song and a slow song to lead children into praise and worship. It works well to talk to the children about what worship is and why it's important before you enter into this time. You can have a children's praise team, but until they understand leading praise and worship, have an adult leader or yourself be the worship leader.

Object Lessons:

1. 5 Finger Prayer

Supplies needed: none

Show how to use the fingers on your hand to illustrate how to remember the parts of the Lord's prayer.

Thumb - Praise

Our Father who is in heaven, Hallowed be Your name

The prayer starts out by praising God for who He is. Just as we can't do anything without our thumb, we can't do anything without God.

Pointer Finger - I Want What God Wants

Your kingdom come. Your will be done, On earth as it is in heaven.

Pointing your pointer finger toward Heaven, teach children to pray, "I want what God wants."

Middle Finger - Biggest Chunk of Prayer

Give us this day our daily bread.

Our third finger is our biggest finger, just like praying about our needs and the needs of others usually takes the longest time in prayer.

Ring Finger - Relationships

And forgive us our debts, as we also have forgiven our debtors.

The ring finger represents relationships. We ask God to forgive our sins so we have a right relationship with God. We ask Him to help us forgive those who have offended us so we have a right relationship with others.

Pinkie Finger – Small Problem

And do not lead us into temptation, but deliver us from evil.

Your pinky finger is your smallest finger. That's why we use it when we ask God to deliver us from temptation and the evil one. Compared to God, the devil is very small.

Fist – End with Praise and Power

For Yours is the kingdom and the power and the glory forever. Amen.

Just as we started with praise and worship, we end with praise and worship because God gives us power when we praise Him during our prayers.

2. Object Lesson: How to Pray

Supplies needed: none

You can illustrate this as a skit with 2 children or adults, or you can demonstrate it yourself. The examples come from Matthew 6 and Luke 18.

Jesus didn't only teach the disciples what to pray for. He also taught them how to pray. He taught them the attitude they should have when they pray. I'm going to give you some examples Jesus gave when he taught the disciples how to pray. See if you can figure out which one is the right way.

After each example is over, have your students guess which is the right way and tell why.

Example 1: Person one prays loud and uses a lot of thee's and thou's to impress. Person two prays humbly.

Example 2: Person one says the same thing over and over. You could use a rosary prayer or even the Lord's prayer, but have the person chant it many times. Person two praises God and asks Him to meet a certain need.

Example 3: Person one says, "Lord, I thank you I'm not like all of these sinners. Their robbers and bad people. I am a good person who gives in the offering, prays every day, and even fasts once a week. Person two says, "Lord, I am a sinner. Please forgive me."

Message: We Can Boldly Pray

Supplies Needed: rock, rubber snake, bread, toy fish

Sometimes, children have a hard time praying because they don't know how to pray. That's why we had this lesson about how to pray, but sometimes children worry about praying the wrong way, or they think they're not good enough to pray. That's not true. God wants us to talk to Him. He's always with us to help us through anything we might go through. He loves us. In the Bible, Jesus talks about how if we ask our parents for a fish sandwich (show fish), they won't give us a snake instead. (show snake) If we ask them for a piece of toast or bread, they won't give us a rock to eat instead. God loves us even more than our parents do. When we talk to God by praying, He wants to answer our prayers by giving us what is best for us. Even if we don't say the right words or remember all the ways to pray, we can still talk to God anytime we want to. He wants to hear from us.

For response time, encourage each student to separate from the others and find a place to pray privately.

Small Group Activity: Prayer List

Supplies needed: notebook or journal for each child, tabs to separate the notebook into the followed sections: praise, God's will, needs, forgiveness, protection

Give each child a notebook with tabs already labeled. These are their prayer journals. Explain how they can use these journals to write down their prayers and requests. Younger children can draw picture illustrating their prayers.

Tab 1 (Praise): Write down things we praise God for.

Tab 2 (God's Will): Write down prayer requests we know are God's will.

Tab 3 (Needs): Write down needs for us and others.

Tab 4 (Forgiveness): Write down things we need forgiven for and things we need to forgive others for.

Tab 5 (Protection): Write down temptations and situations we need protection from.

Give children time to write some of their prayer requests in their journals. Encourage them to put a star in front of each request as it is answered. Keep the prayer journals at the church until after the four lessons on prayer. Then the students can work on their journals each week.

Lesson 2 – Don't Worry – Pray!

Focus Point: When you are worried, pray about it.

Goal: Students will learn they can give their worries to God

Verse of the Day: Philippians 4:6 (ICB) *"Do not worry about anything. But pray and ask God for everything you need. And when you pray, always give thanks."*

Supplies Needed:

- doctor puppet or doctor costume for skit
- portable toolbox with various tools
- Tyler the Power Tool Guy Skit: Tyler wears a portable toolbox or toolbelt with various tools and is dressed in blue jeans and a plaid shirt, etc.
- power screwdriver
- post it notes or papers with scotch tape
- chairs in a circle
- Bible story: (optional) fake chains or ropes, toy swords, angel costume
- beanbag or soft ball
- backpack
- lots of heavy books, bricks, or rocks
- jar with lid
- pitcher with water
- dishwashing liquid
- food coloring
- tray
- vegetable oil
- 3 clear cups
- marker

Opening: *Power Tools Countdown* (optional) or *Power Tools* Slide

Welcome: Don't Worry - Pray

Supplies needed: post it notes or papers with scotch tape

Welcome children. I've been so worried about today's lesson, but then I remembered something very important. I don't have to worry about anything, because I can give my worries to God in prayer.

Ask the children for prayer requests. Write each prayer request on a separate piece of paper for game time later.

Prayer: Ask a child to pray over the service.

Rules: (use rules slide) Go over the 5 Ups Rules.

Go over the *5 Ups Rules*: 1. Sit up straight. 2. Listen up. 3. Hush up. 4. Don't get up and run around or go to the bathroom. 5. Worship Up! (stand up and participate during praise and worship)

Theme or Activity Songs: Choose one of two fast moving activity or theme songs that go with the curriculum.

Game Time: Musical Prayers (use game time slide)

Supplies needed: chairs in a circle, prayer needs from welcome time taped to the chairs. Have extra needs like children who don't have enough to eat or missionaries in case there aren't enough requests.

Play this game like musical chairs except make sure there are enough chairs for each student. When the music stops, have each student pray for the need taped to the chair he or she sat in.

Memory Verse Skit: (use Prayer Power Lesson 2, slide A)

Supplies needed: doctor puppet or doctor costume for skit

Doctor Word: Hi kids. I'm Doctor Word. I'm called that because I'm a doctor and because I love the Word of God. Being a doctor is a stressful job. I used to worry about all my patients, especially the ones who were very sick. I wouldn't be able to eat or sleep because I was so worried about them. Before long, I started getting stomach aches from the stress. That's when I read today's memory verse. Philippians 4:6 (ICB) says, *Do not worry about anything. But pray and ask God for everything you need. And when you pray, always give thanks.* After that, I stopped worrying about my patients. I would ask God to heal each of them and to give me the wisdom to treat their medical problems, and I would thank Him for answering my prayers. I started being able to eat and sleep again, and God would show me what to do with some of my patients. There were some patients He even miraculously healed without me having to treat them. I'm so glad I learned to stop worrying and to pray.

Offering: Treasures in Heaven (use Prayer Power Lesson 2, slide B)

Sometimes people call our money and possessions treasures. They call them that because they are valuable. God doesn't mind us having money and possessions, but He wants us to consider Him the most valuable thing in our lives. When we do that, we'll want to give in the offering to build the Kingdom of God. Matthew 6:21 (NIV) says, "For where your treasure is, there your heart will be also."

Have a child pray over the offering.

Skit: Tyler the Power Tool Guy Doesn't Have the Tool He Needs

Supplies needed: Tyler has a portable toolbox or toolbelt with various tools and is dressed in blue jeans and a plaid shirt, etc. If you use a girl in the skit, have her dress the same and call her Tyler the Power Tool Gal.

Tyler the Power Tool Guy: (Comes in muttering) What am I going to do? I just don't know what to do.

Leader: Hello, Tyler the Power Tool Guy. You look worried. Is anything wrong?

Tyler: Yes, something's wrong, and I just don't know what to do. If I don't get the outlet replaced soon, I'll probably lose my job. Then I won't be able to pay my rent, and I'll probably end up losing my apartment and living in my car. No, that won't work. I owe payments on my car too, so I'll probably be out living on the street in no time. Tyler, the Power Tool Guy, will be homeless. I never thought it would come to this.

Leader: Calm down, Tyler. Why can't you replace the outlet?

Tyler: I went to seven power tool stores. Not one of them has a Phillips Number Two bit for my power screwdriver. I need that attachment to replace the outlet. What am I going to do?

Leader: Your problem reminds me of our lesson today.

Tyler: You're teaching the kids how to replace an outlet. I can teach them that. That is if I had the right power tool.

Leader: I'm teaching these boys and girls what to do if they have a problem.

Tyler: Maybe I need that lesson because I sure have a problem.

Leader: The first part of the lesson is Don't Worry.

Tyler: Don't worry? That's easy for you to say. You don't need to replace an outlet when you don't have the right tools. You're not the one who's going to lose his job and become homeless.

Leader: Wait, Tyler. You don't understand. The most important part of the lesson is to pray. God knows what you need before you need it, and He knows how to help you.

Tyler: Just pray huh?

Leader: That's right. Don't worry – Pray.

Tyler: I'll try it. (bows his head and folds his hands together) Lord, I need to change the outlet box to keep my job, and I don't have a number two Phillips attachment for my electric screwdriver. Please, help me. (lifts head) Now what.

Leader: God will answer your prayer. Keep praying and thanking Him for the answer.

Tyler: That doesn't make any sense, but I'll try it. I don't know what else to do.

Leader: You'll see. Prayer works.

Tyler: I have to go now. I haven't tried Lowes or Home Depot yet. Maybe they have what I need. Even if they don't, I'll keep praying and try not to worry. Bye.

Verse of the Day: Philippians 4:6 (ICB) says, *Do not worry about anything. But pray and ask God for everything you need. And when you pray, always give thanks.*

Memory Verse Talk: (use Prayer Power Lesson 2, slide A)

Have you ever been worried about something? Worry is not a good feeling, but we all do it. Our memory verse for today tells us what to do if we're worried about something. It say's "Do not worry about anything." That's easy to say, but it's hard to do. Can you stop worrying just because someone tells you to stop. Allow children to answer. *I can't either. I'm glad the Scripture didn't just tell us not to worry. It tells us what to do instead.*

"But pray and ask God for everything you need. And when you pray, always give thanks." So, if I'm worried about something, instead of wringing my hands, dwelling on it, and worrying even more, I can pray and ask God for everything I need. Isn't it awesome that the God of the universe wants me to come to Him when I have a problem and tell Him what I need?

When I think about how much God cares about me, it's easy to do the next part of the verse. "And when you pray, always give thanks." Let's take a moment and give God thanks because He cares so much for us. Lead the children into a prayer of thanks.

Memory Verse Activity: (use Prayer Power Lesson 2, slide A)

Supplies needed: none

Have your students say the memory verse in different ways such as the following.

Whisper the verse.

Shout the verse.

Say the verse frightened.

Say the verse confidently.

Say the verse with a squeaky voice.

Sing the verse.

Bible Story: Peter Escapes from Prison

(Acts 12:1-17)

Supplies needed: (optional) fake chains or ropes, toy swords, angel costume

Tell the story in Acts 12:1-17. Have the children act out the story as you tell it with the following characters: Peter, King Herod, 1-4 soldiers depending on the size of your group, angel, Rhoda. All others depict the praying church. Tell the children what to do for each part of the story.

King Herod hated Christians. He even had James, one of the disciples, killed. Then he arrested Peter. Have King Herod order Peter be arrested. Have guards arrest Peter and chain him or bind him with ropes or chains. *Herod planned to kill Peter in the morning.*

Peter could have worried all night, but he trusted God to answer his prayers, so he went to sleep. Have Peter go to sleep in the middle of the guards.

The church was worried about Peter, so they had an all-night prayer meeting and prayed for Peter.

Have the church say, "Lord, save Peter from Herod."

In the middle of the night, an angel appeared in the prison. Angel appears and says, "Peter, wake up." *Peter was so sound asleep that the angel had to shake him awake.* Angel shakes Peter. *The chain fell off Peter, and he followed the angel out of the prison.* Have Peter do so. *The guards didn't even notice.*

Once Peter was a couple of blocks away, the angel disappeared. Have the angel leave. *Peter was astonished because he thought he was dreaming.* Have Peter look surprised. *He decided to go to the house where the Christians were praying.* Peter walks around, and Christians say, "Lord rescue Peter."

Peter knocked on the door. Have Peter knock. *Rhoda, a girl who had been praying, answered it and was so surprised and overjoyed that she closed the door in Peter's face and went to tell the others Peter was outside.* Have Rhoda do so. *The church people were surprised too, but at first, they didn't believe Rhoda.* Have the church people say things like, "You're dreaming. Maybe it's his ghost."

Peter kept knocking, and eventually, Rhoda let him in. Then he told the people what happened.

Peter didn't worry. He prayed. The church worried about Peter getting killed, so they prayed instead of worrying. God answered their prayers and rescued Peter.

Praise Lesson: Beanbag of Thanksgiving

Supplies needed: beanbag or soft ball

The last part of our memory verse says, "And when you pray, always give thanks." We're going to take some time to do that. This is our beanbag (ball) or thanksgiving. I'm going to throw the beanbag. If you catch it, say something you are thankful to God for.

Throw the beanbag to as many children as you like. If you have enough students, give each of them a chance to catch the beanbag.

Praise and Worship: Choose a couple of fast song and a slow song to lead children into praise and worship. It works well to talk to the children about what worship is and why it's important before you enter into this time. You can have a children's praise team, but until they understand leading praise and worship, have an adult leader or yourself be the worship leader.

Object Lesson:

1. **Object Lesson: Let God Carry Your Burdens** (use Prayer Power Lesson 2, slide C)

Supplies needed: backpack; lots of heavy books, bricks, or rocks

Show slide and read the following verse.

Matthew 11:28 says, "Come to me, all you who are weary and burdened, and I will give you rest.

Choose the strongest boy in the class for this demonstration, or choose a teenager in the church to help you. Have him place the open backpack on his back. As you talk, continue to place heavy objects in the backpack.

There are many worries we carry in life. Even at your young age, worry is a part of life. For instance, you have to worry about homework and making good grades. Sometimes you might worry about making friends or having people like you. Some kids have to worry about moving away or their parents divorcing. Sometimes, there are even more things to worry about like someone abusing you or an illness you, your family, or a friend might have. Or you might have to deal with a bully who wants to beat you up or a teacher who doesn't like you. These are big worries. Even adults worry when things like these happen. These worries can weigh you down like this heavy backpack.

Ask the boy if the backpack is heavy. Ask him if he would like you to take away some of the weight.

Jesus cares about you so much, He wants to carry your burdens for you. That's what this verse is all about.

Instruct the boy to take off the backpack. Have him take each book, rock, or brick out and say, "Lord, I give this burden to you." After he has done that for each book, have him place the bookbag back on his back. Ask him if the backpack is lighter than before.

That's the way it is with each worry that burdens us down. As we pray and give that burden to God, He carries it for us because He care for us.

2. Object Lesson: When Worry Bubbles Up

Supplies needed: jar with lid, pitcher, water, dishwashing liquid, food coloring, tray

Preparation: Fill jar ¼ full with water. Fill pitcher completely with water and add food coloring. Place tray under jar to catch excess water.

Sometimes it's hard to stop worrying even when we do pray. Pour a good amount of dishwashing liquid in the jar and close with lid. Shake the jar vigorously while you are talking. The jar should fill with bubbles.

We might want to stop worrying. We might even pray about what we're worried about, but the more we think about it, the more worried we get. No matter what we do, we can't keep worry from bubbling up inside of us. Mention worries the students might have.

Nothing we do can get rid of the worry in our hearts. Open the jar and start to pour the colored water in the jar. *But if we ask the Holy Spirit to fill us with His peace and His joy and His love, He will take away the worry and fill us with the Holy Spirit.* Keep filling the jar until it overflows and there are no more bubbles left in the jar. *The more we are filled with God, the less worry we will have. When we pray, we want to not only give our worries to God, we want to ask Him to replace those worries with more of the Holy Spirit.*

Optional Video: Knock, Knock

Show **Knock, Knock** video found in Power Tools Additional Downloadable Resources

Matthew 7:7 (NIV) says, "Ask and it will be given to you; seek and you will find; knock and the door will be opened to you." Sometimes when we pray, it doesn't feel like God is answering us, but just as

the man in the video did, God wants us to keep on asking, seeking, and knocking. He will answer our prayers.

Message: Worry and Prayer Don't Mix

(use Prayer Power Lesson 2, slides A & D)

Supplies needed: water, food coloring, vegetable oil, 3 clear cups, marker

Preparation: Use the marker to label cups worry, prayer, and Holy Spirit.

Mix food coloring with water and pour it in the first cup. *This cup represents worry.*

Pour oil in the second cup. *This cup represents prayer.*

Now let's see what happens when we combine worry and prayer. Pour both the water and the oil in the third cup. Wait a moment. Since water and oil don't mix, the oil will rise to the top above the water.

When we pray and give our worries to God in prayer, the Holy Spirit takes over and covers our worries. The more we pray and the closer we get to God, the more the Holy Spirit will cover us with His peace.

Show slide A. *Our memory verse, Philippians 4:6 (ICB), says, Do not worry about anything. But pray and ask God for everything you need. And when you pray, always give thanks. The next verse tells why we don't need to worry when we pray.*

Show slide D. *Philippians 4:7 (ICB) says, "And God's peace will keep your hearts and minds in Christ Jesus. The peace that God gives is so great that we cannot understand it."*

When we pray, the Holy Spirit covers our hearts and minds with His peace, peace so great we can't understand it. When that happens, we won't worry. Instead, we'll thank God. Worry and prayer don't mix when the Holy Spirit gives us His peace.

For response time, lay hands on each of your student's heads and pray for God's peace to overcome any worries they might have.

Small Group Chat: Send Worries to God

Supplies needed: helium filled balloons, ribbon, marker

Have a ribbon tied to each helium-filled balloon. Give each child a balloon and instruct that child to hold onto the ribbon until you say differently. Ask each child something he worries about and write it on that student's balloon. Abbreviate if you need to. Have extra balloons in case a balloon break or a student accidently lets go.

These balloons represent things we worry about. We're going to take the balloons outside. Hold onto the ribbon attached to your balloons. Don't let them go.

Take the students outside and have them stand in a circle.

Philippians 4:13 (ICB) says, "Do not worry about anything. But pray and ask God for everything you need. And when you pray, always give thanks." That's what we are going to do. Repeat after me. "Lord, take this worry from me. I give it to you." Now let go of the balloons.

Give your students a few moments to let the balloons float away. *Just as these balloons floated up to the sky, God will take our worries away when we pray, and He'll give us His peace.*

Lead your students in a prayer thanking God.

Lesson 3 – FAITH Prayers

Focus Point: Faith is the secret ingredient of prayer.

Goal: Students will learn they need to add faith to their prayers.

Verse of the Day: Matthew 17:20 (NIV) … *If you have faith as small as a mustard seed, you can say to this mountain, 'Move from here to there,' and it will move. Nothing will be impossible for you.*

Supplies Needed:

- doctor puppet or doctor costume for skit
- portable toolbox with various tools
- Tyler the Power Tool Guy Skit: Tyler wears a portable toolbox or toolbelt with various tools and is dressed in blue jeans and a plaid shirt, etc.
- power screwdriver
- balls or balloons
- mustard seeds (You can purchase these at any spice shop or in the spice section of the Grocery store. If you don't have a mustard seed, any small seed will do.)
- beanbag or soft ball
- Signs with the following written on them with a colorful marker: TIRED, EXCITED, JESUS IS HERE, BOO, THAT'S DIFFERENT, I WILL HEAL HIM, AMAZING
- Blindfold
- clear cup
- baking soda
- vinegar
- tray
- 2 Styrofoam or colored cups
- slush powder (available online or at magic shops)

Opening: *Power Tools Countdown* (optional) or *Power Tools* Slide

Welcome:

Welcome. I hope you've all been praying and writing prayer requests in your journals. Today, we're going to talk about the secret ingredient of prayer. What do you think that ingredient might be? Allow the children to answer, but don't comment on their answers. *Those were all good answers. One of them might have even been the correct one. But I can't tell you what it is. It's a secret.*

I'm just kidding. This is a secret God wants everyone to know. The secret ingredient of prayer is FAITH.

Prayer: Ask a child to pray over the service.

Rules: (use rules slide) Go over the 5 Ups Rules.

Go over the *5 Ups Rules*: 1. Sit up straight. 2. Listen up. 3. Hush up. 4. Don't get up and run around or go to the bathroom. 5. Worship Up! (stand up and participate during praise and worship)

Theme or Activity Songs: Choose one of two fast moving activity or theme songs that go with the curriculum.

Game Time: Ball Toss (use game time slide)

Supplies needed: balls or balloons

Have the students arrange themselves in a circle. The goal of the game is not to let any balls fall on the floor. Students will work together to keep the balls in the air. If a ball falls to the floor, the game is over although you can play the game more than once.

Start by throwing one ball into the circle. Once the students keep that ball in the air, throw in another ball. Keep throwing in balls, one at a time, until the game is over.

When the game is over, ask the students how difficult it was to keep the balls in the air when you kept throwing in more balls. This is almost impossible to keep up for long, but God does the impossible. That's why we can have faith in Him when we pray.

Memory Verse Skit: (use Prayer Power Lesson 3, slide A)

Supplies needed: doctor puppet or doctor costume for skit

Doctor Word: Hi kids. I'm Doctor Word. I'm called that because I'm a doctor and because I love the Word of God. Sometimes being a doctor and treating patients is almost impossible. That's even more true when a patient isn't getting better. I had a patient like that a couple of weeks ago. After doing all I could, I knew the patient was going to die of Covid. I used every medical technique I could think of, but nothing helped. That's when I read today's memory verse. Matthew 17:20 (NIV) says, *"If you have faith as small as a mustard seed, you can say to this mountain, 'Move from here to there,' and it will move. Nothing will be impossible for you."* I decided I wanted that kind of faith, so I spoke to the Covid virus invading my patient's body and told it to leave. I commanded my patient to be completely healed in Jesus' name. At first, nothing happened, but the next day when I was making rounds, I found out that my patient was completely better. He was miraculously healed and got to go home from the hospital that very day. From that point on, I knew faith is the secret ingredient that answers my prayers.

Offering: The Secret Ingredient of Giving

Whenever I give in the offering, I give in faith. First, I give knowing that God blesses me with money to give. Second, I know that God will use the money I give to build the Kingdom of God. So, faith isn't only a secret ingredient for prayer, it's a secret ingredient for offering as well.

Skit: Tyler the Power Tool Guy Doesn't Have the Tool He Needs

Supplies Needed: Tyler has a portable toolbox or toolbelt with various tools and is dressed in blue jeans and a plaid shirt, etc. If you use a girl in the skit, have her dress the same and call her Tyler the Power Tool Gal.

Tyler the Power Tool Guy: (Comes in muttering) It didn't work. Now, I don't know what to do.

Leader: I don't understand. What didn't work?

Tyler: Prayer. I prayed God would help me find a Phillips number 2 bit for my power screwdriver, but it didn't work. I can't find the bit anywhere. I knew it wouldn't work before I even tried. Now, what am I going to do?

Leader: Wait a minute. Did you say you knew it wasn't going to work before you even tried praying?

Tyler: Yep, and I was right. Prayer is useless.

Leader: I agree.

Tyler: You do? But you're the one who wanted me to pray about it.

Leader: I'm not saying prayer is useless, but the way you prayed, you might as well have not even bothered.

Tyler: I don't get it. You mean there was a certain way I was supposed to pray?

Leader: That's right. There's a secret ingredient to prayer you didn't use. That's why your prayers didn't work.

Tyler: How in the world is that supposed to help me if it's a secret.

Leader: This is the kind of secret God wants everyone to know.

Tyler: I don't understand. If it's a secret, why would God want everyone to know?

Leader: That's a good question, but I don't have an answer.

Tyler: So, what's the secret?

Leader: Faith. Nothing is impossible for God, but we have to have faith that He'll answer our prayers.

Tyler: That won't help me. I just became a Christian a few weeks ago. I don't have a lot of faith like people who have been saved a long time.

Leader: You don't need a lot of faith. Matthew 17:20 (NIV) says, "If you have faith as small as a mustard seed, you can say to this mountain, 'Move from here to there,' and it will move. Nothing will be impossible for you."

Tyler: As small as a mustard seed? I saw a mustard seed once. It's really tiny.

Leader: Yes, it is. God doesn't require us to have this great big faith. He only wants us to have faith in Him. When we do that, we'll be amazed by what God will do. Nothing is impossible with Him.

Tyler: If I only need a tiny bit of faith, I'll try it. I have to go now. I want to try praying using my secret ingredient – faith.

(Exits)

Verse of the Day: Matthew 17:20 (NIV) … *If you have faith as small as a mustard seed, you can say to this mountain, 'Move from here to there,' and it will move. Nothing will be impossible for you.*

Memory Verse Talk: (use Prayer Power Lesson 3, slide A)

Supplies needed: mustard seed (If you don't have a mustard seed, any small seed will do.)

Matthew 17:20 (NIV) says, "If you have faith as small as a mustard seed, you can say to this mountain, 'Move from here to there,' and it will move. Nothing will be impossible for you." Have any of you ever seen a mustard seed? Show the mustard seed. *Mustard seeds are the smallest seeds there are. Why do you suppose God would want us to have faith as small as a mustard seed? I would think He would say, "If you have faith as big as a mountain, you can tell the mountain to be removed." But that's not what God says. Our faith only has to be a big as a mustard seed. God doesn't expect us to have some giant faith for our prayers to be answered. What He does want is for us to trust in Him. When we do that, He will answer our prayers in miraculous ways.*

Memory Verse Activity: If You...

If the following statements fit, students must stand and recite the verse:

Did you brush your teeth today?

Do you have blue eyes?

Do you have brown eyes?

Are you wearing green?

Are you wearing blue?

Did your parents drive you to church?

Come up with other questions until everyone has a chance, then make one more statement.

Do you have faith as big as a mustard seed? Encourage everyone to stand for this question.

Bible Story: Amazing Faith

(Luke 7:1-10)

Supplies Needed: Signs with the following written on them with a colorful marker: TIRED, EXCITED, JESUS IS HERE, BOO, THAT'S DIFFERENT, I WILL HEAL HIM, AMAZING. Write in pencil on the back what each sign says so you can easily find the right sign, or make duplicates of some of the signs so you can place them in order.

Show the signs as you tell the story. Instruct your students to say what the signs read with the feeling they convey.

A long time ago, after Jesus finished preaching to a large crowd of people, He came down from the mountain and headed to the town of Capernaum. Show TIRED sign.

News spread that Jesus was coming to Capernaum. Show EXCITED sign. *They were very excited. They knew Jesus had healed many sick people and had even raised people from the dead.*

They shouted, "Jesus is here." Jesus is here. Show JESUS IS HERE sign. *They shared the news with all of their friends. People filled the streets to try to get a glimpse of Him.*

Before long, a Roman centurion heard the news. Show BOO sign. *In that day, Romans suppressed the Jewish people and taxed them unfairly.* Show BOO sign. *They even took away their rights to be fairly treated.* Show BOO Sign. *This man wasn't only a Roman, he was a centurion, basically a captain in the Roman army.* Show BOO Sign.

But this centurion was different than most Romans. He love God and even donated money to build a synagogue, basically a Jewish church, for the people of that town. Show THAT'S DIFFERENT sign. *He even cared for his servants and treated them well.* Show THAT'S DIFFERENT sign. *One of his servants was sick. The centurion didn't want to leave his side, but he knew Jesus was the only one who could help the man. He sent for one of his officers and asked the man to send for the Jews who were the leaders of the synagogue he'd built.*

As soon as the leaders came to his house, the centurion said, "Go quickly and find Jesus. Beg Him to come and heal my servant." Most Jews wouldn't even go to a Roman's home, let alone help him, but because the leaders knew the centurion had helped them, did what he said. Show THAT'S DIFFERENT sign.

It wasn't easy for the men. They had to push their way through the crowded streets. Everyone in the town had flooded the streets saying, "Jesus is here." Show JESUS IS HERE sign. *Eventually the leaders found Jesus and pushed through the crowd to get near Him.* Show JESUS IS HERE sign.

They pleaded with Him to come with them and heal the centurion's dying servant. "If anyone deserves your help, it is this man," they said. "He loves the Jews and even paid personally to build us a synagogue."

I wonder if Jesus thought about how unusual it was for Jewish leaders to plead for a Roman centurion. Show THAT'S DIFFERENT sign. *I wonder if He was thinking about the sermon He'd just preached about loving your enemies.*

In any case, Jesus decided to go to the Roman centurion's house and heal his servant. Show I WILL HEAL HIM sign. *He followed the leaders of the synagogue through the crowded streets to the centurion's home. He probably had to push through the excited crowd to go there.* Show EXCITED sign.

When Jesus was almost to the centurion's home, a group of the centurion's friends arrived with a message for Jesus.

The message said, "Sir, do not trouble yourself to come to my home, for I am unworthy for you to enter under my roof or even to come and meet you. Just speak a word, and I know my dear servant will be healed." The Roman centurion had so much faith in Jesus that he didn't even need Him to come to his home. He knew Jesus would heal his servant. Show I WILL HEAL HIM sign.

The message also said, "I know how it is, for I receive orders from my superior officers and I give orders to those under my authority. All I have to say is, 'Go!' and they go, or 'Come!' and they come, and to my servant, 'Do this or that' and he does it. So if you just say, 'Be healed,' my servant will be made well." Show I WILL HEAL HIM sign.

When Jesus heard the centurion's words, he was amazed. Show AMAZING sign. *Jesus turned around and said to the crowd that was following Him, "Never among all the Jews in Israel have I met a man with faith like this."* Show AMAZING sign. *There's only one person in the Bible who amazed Jesus because of his faith. It wasn't one of His disciples or a Jewish leader. It was a Roman centurion.* Show THAT'S DIFFERENT sign.

After that, the centurion came to Jesus. Jesus turned to him and said, "Go your way. Just as you have believed, it will be done." Show I WILL HEAL HIM sign.

When the centurion and his friends returned to the house, they found the servant had been healed at the same time Jesus had promised.

I don't know about you, but I want to have the kind of faith that amazes Jesus. I want amazing faith. Show AMAZING sign.

Praise Lesson: Beanbag of Thanksgiving

Supplies needed: beanbag or soft ball

We're going to spend some time every week during this series thanking God. This is our beanbag (ball) or thanksgiving. I'm going to throw the beanbag. If you catch it, say something you are thankful to God for.

Throw the beanbag to as many children as you like. If you have enough students, give each of them a chance to catch the beanbag.

Praise and Worship: Choose a couple of fast song and a slow song to lead children into praise and worship. It works well to talk to the children about what worship is and why it's important before you enter into this time. You can have a children's praise team, but until they understand leading praise and worship, have an adult leader or yourself be the worship leader.

Object Lessons:

1. What is Faith (use Prayer Power Lesson 3, slide B)

Supplies needed: blindfold, obstacles

Sometimes, we hear a certain word, but we don't really know what it means. That is sometimes the case with faith, but the Bible tells us what faith means. Show slide and read verse. *Hebrews 11:1 (NIV) says, "Now faith is confidence in what we hope for and assurance about what we do not see." In other words, faith is the confidence we have in God before we see the proof. I'm going to give you an example of faith.*

Choose a student who is known for listening to instructions. Set up obstacles along the path you want the student to take. Have the student go to the back of the room. Blindfold him, and spin him around three times. Tell him that if he listens to your instructions and does them, no harm will come to him, and he'll make it to the front of the room.

Give the student instructions to avoid the obstacles and go to the front of the room. When he gets there, tell him to count slowly to three, then fall back. While he is counting, quietly stand behind him. When he falls back, catch him.

Congratulate the student in having enough faith to listen even when he didn't know you were there to catch him.

2. Object Lesson: Faith That Pleases God

(Use Prayer Power Lesson 3, slides C & D)

(Mark 9:17-27)

Supplies needed: clear cup, baking soda, vinegar, tray to catch excess water

Did you know that without faith, even your prayers won't please God?

Show slide C. *Hebrews 11:6 (NIV) says, "And without faith it is impossible to please God, because anyone who comes to him must believe that he exists and that he rewards those who earnestly seek him."*

God doesn't answer faithless prayers. So, if we have a hard time believing God will answer our prayers, how do we get enough faith to please God? One way is to ask God to give you faith.

Show slide D. *Hebrews 12:2 (ICB) says, "Let us look only to Jesus. He is the one who began our faith, and he makes our faith perfect."*

There was one man in the Bible during Jesus' time who was worried he didn't have enough faith. He was a father, and his son was tormented by demons who made the boy go into convulsions. The man had asked the disciples to heal the boy, but they couldn't. Then he went to Jesus and asked if Jesus could heal the boy. Jesus said, "Everything is possible for one who believes."

The boy's father knew he didn't have enough faith, but he said, "I believe. Help me overcome my unbelief." Because he asked Jesus to help him have more faith and overcome his unbelief, Jesus rebuked the demon, and the boy was healed. When we pray, we can ask God for the kind of faith that pleases Him.

Pour some baking soda in the clear cup. *Pretend this baking soda is a prayer that doesn't have the secret ingredient of faith. It just sits there and does nothing. Pretend this vinegar is faith. "Lord, please give me the faith I need to please you."* Pour in the vinegar. *God will give us the explosive faith that makes our prayers effective.*

Optional Object Lesson: Building Our Faith

Supplies needed: 2 Styrofoam or colored cups, slush powder (available online or at magic shops)

Preparation: Pour a tablespoon of slush powder into the first cup. Pour a little bit of water in the second cup. Try the experiment before doing it with your students to make sure you have enough slush powder.

Choose a volunteer. Ask the student if he or she trust you. If he says no, choose another volunteer. Have the student stretch out his hand and hold the cup with the slush powder. It is very important the student keeps his hand stretched out so he doesn't see what's in the cup.

Pour the water from the second cup into the first cup. Ask the student again if he trusts you. Tell the student to dump the water on his head. If he doesn't want to, encourage him to trust you. If he won't do it, ask for another volunteer. When the student dumps the water, nothing should come out. Take the cup away immediately so the student doesn't examine it.

Just as (student's name) trusted me when I asked him to do something he didn't want to do, we should have enough faith to trust God to do the impossible.

Message: Building My Faith

(Use Prayer Power Lesson 3, slides E-I)

Show slide E: *In the Book of Jude, the Bible tells us to build our faith. Here are some ways you can do that.*

Show slide F: *Ask God for faith. Remember that all faith starts with God, and He wants to give you the faith you need.*

Show slide G: *Remember that God does the impossible. With God, we can do anything even if our faith is only as big as a mustard seed. There is nothing impossible for God.*

Show slide H: *Learn God's Word. Romans 10:17 (NKJV) says, "So then faith comes by hearing, and hearing by the word of God." The more we learn about God from the Bible, the more faith we'll have.*

Show slide I: *Seek God: Hebrews 11:6 (NIV) says, And without faith it is impossible to please God, because anyone who comes to him must believe that he exists and that he rewards those who earnestly seek him." God doesn't want us to grow our faith for the sake of having great faith. It's more important to seek God than faith. As we seek God, our faith will grow.*

Small Group Chat: Mustard seed bookmark

Supplies needed: cardstock, glue, scissors, markers, stickers, colored pencils, mustard seeds (you can get them in any spice store or the spice department of your groceries store)

Preparation: Cut the blank cardstock paper in to bookmark size strips. For an 8 1/2 by 11 size paper, you should be able to make 5 bookmarks.

Have the children use the supplies to decorate their bookmarks. Encourage them to use mustard seeds as part of their decorations.

While the children are working on their bookmarks, tell a story about when God answered your prayer.

Lesson 4 - Powerful Prayer

Focus Point: Our prayers are powerful.

Goal: Students will learn they can change things through powerful prayers.

Verse of the Day: James 5: 16b (NIV) … *The prayer of a righteous person is powerful and effective.*

Supplies Needed:

- doctor puppet or doctor costume for skit
- portable toolbox with various tools
- Tyler the Power Tool Guy Skit: Tyler wears a portable toolbox or toolbelt with various tools and is dressed in blue jeans and a plaid shirt, etc.
- power screwdriver
- screwdriver
- a package of cookies
- 12 rocks
- 12 small cups of water
- tray to catch water
- flash paper (available at magic shop or online stores)
- Alternative to flash paper (strips of red, orange, and yellow crepe paper, masking tape, scissors)
- beanbag or soft ball
- cellphone
- ornate lamp or bottle
- Optional - energy stick (available at Amazon, WalMart, and other stores)
- water
- food coloring
- vegetable oil
- 3 clear cups
- marker
- mustard seed
- Every Home for Christ World Prayer Map for Kids (Available free by mail from Every Home for Christ Ministries at https://everyhome.org/prayer/prayer-maps/)

Opening: *Power Tools Countdown* (optional) or *Power Tools* Slide

Welcome: Prayer Time

Welcome. For the last three weeks, we've been learning about the power of prayer. Today we're going to talk more about powerful prayers. The best way to learn how to pray powerfully is to pray with your whole being. Sometimes, that means loudly. When I say go, I want you all to begin praying loudly for the next five minutes. I'll watch the clock and tell you when the five minutes is over. Go.

Prayer: Encourage children as they pray for five minutes. If they stop praying, give them suggestions for things to pray about.

Rules: (use rules slide) Go over the 5 Ups Rules.

Go over the *5 Ups Rules*: 1. Sit up straight. 2. Listen up. 3. Hush up. 4. Don't get up and run around or go to the bathroom. 5. Worship Up! (stand up and participate during praise and worship)

Theme or Activity Songs: Choose one of two fast moving activity or theme songs that go with the curriculum.

Game Time: Cookie Time Minute to Win It (use game time slide)

Supplies needed: a package of cookies, Minute to Win It Countdown found in Prayer Power downloadable resources

You might want to ask your students questions about the previous Prayer Power lessons to decide who participates, or if you have a smaller group, everyone could participate.

Explain to the students how the game is played. They'll each place the cookie on their foreheads. They have one minute to eat the cookie and can start when the countdown starts. Here's the catch. They can't use their hands. They have to use the muscles in their faces to get the cookie to their mouths to eat it. If anyone drops the cookie, he is eliminated.

It was almost impossible to eat that cookie in a minute without using your hands, but with God, all things are possible.

Memory Verse Skit: (use Prayer Power Lesson 4, slide A)

Supplies needed: doctor puppet or doctor costume for skit

Doctor Word: Hi kids. I'm Doctor Word. I'm called that because I'm a doctor and because I love the Word of God. Being a doctor is not for weaklings. When I was a resident, sometimes I had to work twenty-four hours at a time with very few breaks. Most of that time, I was on my feet. Then, when I became a doctor, I did full days of surgery. I would go from one surgery to the next with only a fifteen-minute break in between. You need power to be a good doctor. Prayer is the same way. Sometimes Christians believe that all God requires is a short prayer right before we go to bed, and everything will work out fine. While those short prayers are great, Christians who are effective in their prayers know how to pray passionately and powerfully. James 5: 16b (NIV) *"... The prayer of a righteous person is powerful and effective."*

Offering: Powerful Giving

Have you ever heard of powerful giving? In Luke 6:38 (NIV), it says, "Give, and it will be given to you. A good measure, pressed down, shaken together, and running over, will be poured into your lap. For with the measure you use, it will be measured to you." That's powerful. Whatever we give will explode and come back to us in the same measure or with the same power we gave. That doesn't always mean God will bless us with more money, but it does always mean God will bless us.

Skit: Tyler the Power Tool Guy's Prayers are Answered

Supplies Needed: Tyler has a portable toolbox or toolbelt with various tools and is dressed in blue jeans and a plaid shirt, etc. If you use a girl in the skit, have her dress the same and call her Tyler the Power Tool Gal.

Tyler the Power Tool Guy: (Comes in) I'm so happy you taught us about prayer for the last three weeks. Not only did I find out how to pray, but my prayers were answered and my job was saved.

Leader: That's awesome, Tyler. Tell us about it.

Tyler: I was so worried because I couldn't find a Phillip's number 2 bit for my power screwdriver, so I decided to pray. First, I asked God to help me find the bit, but that didn't happen. Then, I decided to pray in faith and power. I told God I didn't believe He wanted me to lose my job, but I couldn't find that bit anywhere. I asked Him to help me know what to do. Then I thanked Him for the answer knowing God wants what is best for me.

Leader: So, what happened?

Tyler: The next day, I went to the Acme Power Tools Store one more time because I believed God would answer my prayer. Usually, Acme Power Tools only sells power tools, but they were having a special sale. They had a display of regular screwdrivers in the front. I found a Phillip's number two and bought it. Not only that, but it was 50% off. I got it for much less than I expected to pay.

Leader: That's awesome. It sounds like your prayer was powerful.

Tyler: Yep. I took the tool to the church and replaced the outlet box in no time. My boss was happy I figured out what to do and even gave me a raise.

Leader: I'm so happy for you. So, are you going to change your name to Tyler the Tool Guy since you aren't using power tools?

Tyler: I wouldn't go that far. I still love my power tools. This was a one-time thing using a manual screwdriver, but I thank God, He showed me what to do. He is a powerful God who answers power prayers.

Leader: That's so true.

(Exits)

Verse of the Day: James 5:16b (NIV) ... *The prayer of a righteous person is powerful and effective.*

Memory Verse Talk: (use Prayer Power Lesson 4, slide A)

Supplies needed: screwdriver

James 5:16b (NIV) says, "... The prayer of a righteous person is powerful and effective." I don't know about you, but I sure want my prayers to be effective. Effective means that something works right.

Show screwdriver. *For instance, this screwdriver is effective if it's the right size to remove a screw or attach it.*

But the verse goes farther. It says our prayers won't just be effective. They'll be powerful. Powerful means having great power or influence. We can pray powerful prayers when we understand that the God we are praying to is Omnipotent. Omnipotent means all powerful. It means nothing is more powerful than God.

There's one requirement in this verse for our prayers to be powerful and effective. Only the prayers of a righteous person are powerful and effective. Righteous means right with God, but nobody is righteous on their own. We are only righteous because Jesus died on the cross for our sins. We can't be righteous on our own. Only God can make us righteous. That means a person who doesn't believe in God or hasn't asked God to forgive their sins isn't righteous. That person's prayers aren't powerful or effective. I'm glad God makes my prayers powerful and effective.

Memory Verse Activity: Simon Says Verse

Have the students stand. Tell them you're going to play a game of Simon Says. If you say, "Simon says," they repeat what you say, but if you don't say, "Simon says," and they repeat it, they have to sit down. Say the first word of the verse. Then say the first and second word. Then say the first, second, and third word. Keep on going. When you are going to say the words correctly, say, "Simon says." Occasionally mess up the verse, but don't say "Simon says," when you plan to mess it up.

When the game is finished, tell everyone still standing that they won. It doesn't matter how many winners there are. The important thing is they all learn the verse.

Bible Story: Elijah and His Powerful Prayers (use Prayer Power Lesson 4, slide B)

(1 Kings 18:16-39)

Supplies Needed: 12 rocks, 12 small cups of water, tray to catch water, flash paper (available at magic shop or online stores), alternative to flash paper (strips of red, orange, and yellow crepe paper, masking tape, scissors)

Preparation for crepe paper fire: Cut strips of crepe paper. Tape on one end with masking tape.

(Show slide B) *James 5: 17 and 18 (NIV), the verses right after our memory verse, says, "Elijah was a human being, even as we are. He prayed earnestly that it would not rain, and it did not rain on the land for three and a half years. Again, he prayed, and the heavens gave rain, and the earth produced its crops."*

Even though Elijah was a normal person, it sounds like he prayed powerfully. Imagine being able to pray and stop the rain for three years, then being able to pray and start the rain back up. I'm going to tell you another powerful prayer Elijah made.

In those days, King Ahab and his wife, Jezebel, were evil. They encouraged the Jewish people to worship false gods. The people would go to the Temple and worship God, but they also worship the false gods. It's like Christian today who go to church on Sunday and worship God, but the rest of the week, they'll do things God isn't pleased with, or they'll go along with their teachers and friends and agree with things the Bible says are wrong. So Elijah's time wasn't that different than things today.

Elijah challenged King Ahab to a contest on Mount Carmel. He told the king to bring 450 prophets of Baal and 400 prophets of Asherah. That was 850 people on the king's side and Elijah on God's side In 2 Kings 18:21 (NIV), "Elijah went before the people and said, 'How long will you waver between two opinions? If the Lord is God, follow him; but if Baal is God, follow him.'"

Elijah then told the prophets of Baal to lay a sacrifice on an altar and he would do the same. He told them whoever called fire from Heaven to burn up the sacrifice, his God is the real God. He even told them they could go first.

The prophets of Baal and Asherah cried loudly for their gods to bring fire from Heaven until about Noon. When that didn't work, they cut themselves and danced around. By the time they were done, they were a bloody mess.

During all this time, Elijah mocked them. He would say things like, "Shout louder. Maybe your god is daydreaming, or maybe he took a long trip. Maybe he's asleep. Shout loud enough to wake him. Maybe he went to the bathroom. Maybe that's why he doesn't answer.

No matter what these prophets did, nothing happened.

Then Elijah said that it was his turn. He took twelve stones and built an altar. Place the 12 rocks on a table to build and altar. *Then he put the sacrifice on it, but that's not all he did. He told them to fill four buckets and pour them over the altar.* Pour four cups of water over the rocks. *Then he told them to pour four more buckets over the altar.* Pour four cups of water over the rocks. *They did so. A third time, he told them to pour four buckets over the altar, and they did.* Pour four cups of water over the rocks. *The water poured off the altar and filled the trench Elijah had dug.*

Then Elijah prayed a short, but powerful, prayer. He said in I Kings: 18:36-37 (NIV), "Lord, the God of Abraham, Isaac and Israel, let it be known today that you are God in Israel and that I am your servant and have done all these things at your command. Answer me, Lord, answer me, so these people will know that you, Lord, are God, and that you are turning their hearts back again."

As you are saying this prayer, have fire come down from Heaven by lighting the flash paper or dropping the crepe paper fire.

The fire not only consumed the sacrifice, it caused the water to dry up. The people were amazed and fill on their faces crying out that the Lord is the real God.

Elijah trusted God and prayed, and God answered powerfully. We can pray powerfully when we understand that nothing is impossible with God.

Praise Lesson: Beanbag of Thanksgiving

Supplies needed: beanbag or soft ball

We're going to spend some time every week during this series thanking God. This is our beanbag (ball) or thanksgiving. I'm going to throw the beanbag. If you catch it, say something you are thankful to God for.

Throw the beanbag to as many children as you like. If you have enough students, give each of them a chance to catch the beanbag.

Praise and Worship: Choose a couple of fast song and a slow song to lead children into praise and worship. It works well to talk to the children about what worship is and why it's important before you enter into this time. You can have a children's praise team, but until they understand leading praise and worship, have an adult leader or yourself be the worship leader.

Object Lessons:

1. **Pray With Confidence** (use Prayer Power Lesson 4, slide C)

Supplies needed: cellphone

Show cellphone. *I use this phone when I want to talk to somebody. How many of you have a cellphone?* Have the students answer. *Who do you talk to on the cellphone?* Give the students a chance to answer. *Have you ever tried to call someone, but there wasn't enough reception to hear the person clearly?* Have the students answer.

Tell a story about when you needed to make an important call, but you didn't have any cell phone reception, or you phone died.

Show slide C. *1 John 5:14 (NIV) says, "And this is the confidence that we have toward him, that if we ask anything according to his will he hears us."*

That's an awesome promise. We can pray powerful prayers because we know God hears us. We can have confidence that our phone line to God will always work.

2. **Object Lesson: God Always Answers** (use Prayer Power Lesson 4, slides D, E, and F)

Supplies needed: ornate lamp or bottle

Because we know God always answers our prayers, and because nothing is impossible with God, we can sometimes think of Him as a genie in a bottle. Show lamp or bottle. *We can get to a point where we use God to swoop in and give us whatever we want, then swoop out again. This is a dangerous way to think.*

Remember the Elijah story. God is all powerful. That's why the people who were playing around with worshipping God sometimes and worshipping other gods sometimes fell on their faces. They realized God is the real God, and we are not.

God wants us to pray and come to Him with our requests because He loves us. But whatever God decides to do, and however God decides to answer our prayer is always right because He is God.

We should also remember God doesn't answer every prayer. He only answers prayers prayed by His people, by Christians, but if we are a child of God, we can pray expecting God to answer us. Here are three ways He might answer.

Show slide D. *Sometimes God answers yes. He immediately gives us what we are praying for. This happened with Elijah when he prayed for fire to come down from Heaven.* Talk about a prayer in your life where God answered yes.

Show slide E. *Sometimes God answers no. We don't always know why God answers no. Sometimes*

He tells or shows us, but sometimes we won't know until we get to Heaven. If God says no, that's when we need to trust Him because He's God and we're not. In 2 Samuel 7, King David wanted to build a temple of God. God said no, not because He didn't love David or want the temple, but because He wanted King David's son, Solomon, to build it. King David helped Solomon plan the temple, but King Solomon built it. Talk about a prayer you prayed where God said no.

Show slide F. *Sometimes God answers wait. There are times when God doesn't say yes or no. At those times, He is saying wait. It may be God plans to answer yes, but the time isn't right. Other times, He plans to answer yes, but He wants us to learn to be patient. Then there are times He plans to answer no because He is planning something better, and we don't know that until the better comes along. When the Jewish people were slaves of the Egyptians, they cried out to God for Him to rescue them. God didn't answer their prayers right away. Instead, He made them wait. During the waiting time, He was making Moses ready to become their deliverer.* Tell a time when you had to wait for a prayer to be answered.

Optional Object Lesson: The Power of Praying Together

Supplies needed: energy stick (available online at Amazon and other shops)

In Acts 2, God shows us that it is powerful when a group of believers pray together. Let me show you an illustration of that.

Have the students stand in a circle and hold hands except for two of the students. Hold one of those student's hands, and hold on the one end of the energy stick. Keep the circle broken for now.

God listens and answers our prayers when we pray alone, but when we pray in unity, our prayers become even more powerful. So, let's pray in unity. In a moment, I'm going to give you all something to pray for. If you stop praying, you must let go of the hands of the children next to you.

Give the children a need to pray for. Have the student not holding on to your hand grab hold of the other end of the prayer stick. It should light up. When a child breaks the circle, the stick will stop lighting up.

Just as power went through this energy stick when we were all in unity praying, our prayers are powerful when we all pray together for the same thing.

Message: Powerful Prayer

(Use Prayer Power Lesson 4, slides G-J)

Supplies needed: water, food coloring, vegetable oil, 3 clear cups, mustard seed

Today, we're going to review all the things we talked about in the last four Prayer Power lessons. All four of these things can make our prayers powerful.

Show slide G: The Lord's Prayer

Jesus gave us a pattern for praying. Show this pattern using this object lesson from Prayer Power Lesson 1.

Thumb - Praise

Our Father who is in heaven, Hallowed be Your name

The prayer starts out by praising God for who He is. Just as we can't do anything without our thumb, we can't do anything without God.

Pointer Finger - I Want What God Wants

Your kingdom come. Your will be done, On earth as it is in heaven.

Pointing your pointer finger toward Heaven, teach children to pray, "I want what God wants."

Middle Finger - Biggest Chunk of Prayer

Give us this day our daily bread.

Our third finger is our biggest finger, just like praying about our needs and the needs of others usually takes the longest time in prayer.

Ring Finger - Relationships

And forgive us our debts, as we also have forgiven our debtors.

The ring finger represents relationships. We ask God to forgive our sins so we have a right relationship with God. We ask Him to help us forgive those who have offended us so we have a right relationship with others.

Pinkie Finger – Small Problem

And do not lead us into temptation, but deliver us from evil.

Your pinky finger is your smallest finger. That's why we use it when we ask God to deliver us from temptation and the evil one. Compared to God, the devil is very small.

Fist – End with Praise and Power

For Yours is the kingdom and the power and the glory forever. Amen.

Just as we started with praise and worship, we end with praise and worship because God gives us power when we praise Him during our prayers.

Show slide H: Don't Worry, Pray

Redo Prayer Power Lesson 2 Object Lesson entitled Prayer and Worry Don't Mix found here.

Supplies needed: water, food coloring, vegetable oil, 3 clear cups, marker

Use marker to label cups worry, prayer, and Holy Spirit

Mix food coloring with water and pour it in the first cup. *This cup represents worry.*

Pour oil in the second cup. *This cup represents prayer.*

Now let's see what happens when we combine worry and prayer. Pour both the water and the oil in the third cup. Wait a moment. Since water and oil don't mix, the oil will rise to the top above the water.

When we pray and give our worries to God in prayer, the Holy Spirit takes over and covers our worries. The more we pray and the closer we get to God, the more the Holy Spirit will cover us with His peace.

Show slide I: The Secret Ingredient - Faith.

Supplies needed: mustard seed (If you don't have a mustard seed, any small seed will do.)

Show mustard seed. Then read Matthew 17:20.

Matthew 17:20 (NIV) says, "If you have faith as small as a mustard seed, you can say to this mountain, 'Move from here to there,' and it will move. Nothing will be impossible for you."

Show the mustard seed. Mustard seeds are the smallest seeds there are. Why do you suppose God would want us to have faith as small as a mustard seed? I would think He would say, "If you have faith as big as a mountain, you can tell the mountain to be removed." But that's not what God says. Our faith only has to be a big as a mustard seed. God doesn't expect us to have some giant faith for our prayers to be answered. What He does want is for us to trust in Him. Faith is the secret ingredient of prayer.

Show slide J: Pray Powerfully

Today, we learned that we can boldly come before God and pray powerfully. That's just what we're going to do now.

Response Time:

Have all the students come forward to the altar area. If you have a large group, split them up into sections of four to six students each. In each group, all of the students in that group will pray for each student one at a time. Instruct the students how to pray for each student in the group. Appoint one leader in each group to lay his hand on the student's head. The other students will place their hands on his back. Some students may want to give a prayer requests. If they don't, the other students can pray for God to bless that student and help him know God better.

Play worship music while the students are praying, and monitor the groups in case further instruction is needed.

If you don't have the small group chat, give each child an Every Home for Christ world prayer maps (free at this link - https://everyhome.org/prayer/prayer-maps/)

Small Group Chat: Powerful Prayers

Supplies needed: prayer journals, Every Home for Christ world prayer maps (free at this link - https://everyhome.org/prayer/prayer-maps/)

You can order free prayer maps from Every Home for Christ for each student at this link. https://everyhome.org/prayer/

 Discuss what happened during prayer time. Have the students work in their prayer journals they started during lesson one to end the series on prayer.

Power Tools Part 2: Power of Worship

Part 2: Power of Worship

Created to Worship

Luke 4:8 (NIV) ...*Worship the Lord your God. He is the only one you should serve.*

Worthy of Worship

Psalm 29:2 (NKJV) *Give unto the Lord the glory due to His name; Worship the Lord in the beauty of holiness.*

Worship in Spirit and in Truth

John 4:24 (NKJV) *God is Spirit, and those who worship Him must worship in spirit and truth.*

Enjoying Worship

Psalm 16:11 (NKJV) *You will show me the path of life; In Your presence is fullness of joy; At Your right hand are pleasures forevermore.*

Lesson 1 – Created to Worship

Focus Point: The reason we were created is to worship God.

Goal: Because we were created to worship God, we can only find true satisfaction in Him.

Verse of the Day: Luke 4:8 (NIV) ...*Worship the Lord your God. He is the only one you should serve.*

Supplies Needed:

- doctor puppet or doctor costume for skit
- portable toolbox with various tools
- Tyler the Power Tool Guy Skit: Tyler wears a portable toolbox or toolbelt with various tools and is dressed in blue jeans and a plaid shirt, etc.
- 2 spoons
- 2 hard boiled eggs or tennis balls
- obstacles (optional)
- a variety of power tools (optional - manual tools)
- marker board, chalk board, or blank wall
- scotch tape
- colored sheets of paper
- perfume or spikenard essential oil
- cup
- bottle or pitcher of water
- Lego block or toy house

Opening: *Power Tools Countdown* or *Power Tools* Slide (Available free with registration of this curriculum.)

Welcome: *Welcome to Worship Power, part 2 of Power Tools. For the next few weeks, we will learn about one of the most powerful tools in a Christian's life, the power of worship. We were all created by God to worship Him. That is our primary purpose in life, and we can never truly be satisfied unless we worship God. Worship is something that flows out of us as we encounter God. The more we know God, the more we will want to worship Him, and the more we worship Him, the more we will know God.*

There's no better time to worship God than now. When I say go, for five minutes, let's tell God how worthy He is. You can shout Hallelujah or say you're worthy, or even I love you, Jesus or Praise the Lord..

Tell the students when to start. If your students are not ready for five minutes, start them out at one minute, and build from there.

Prayer: Ask a child to pray over the service.

Rules: (use rules slide) Go over the 5 Ups Rules.

Go over the *5 Ups Rules*: 1. Sit up straight. 2. Listen up. 3. Hush up. 4. Don't get up and run around or go to the bathroom. 5. Worship Up! (stand up and participate during praise and worship)

Theme or Activity Songs: Choose one of two fast moving activity or theme songs that go with the curriculum.

Game Time: Wacky Spoon Race (use game time slide)

Supplies Needed: 2 spoons, 2 hard boiled eggs or tennis balls, obstacles (optional)

What are spoons created for? Allow students to answer. *What are eggs (ping pong balls) created for?* Allow students to answer. *What are people created for?* Allow students to answer. *People can do a lot of things, but the reason they are created is to worship God. Today, we're going to use these spoons and eggs (ping pong balls) for a purpose they aren't created for.*

Have two teams do a relay race. The first student on each team has to balance an egg or ping pong ball on his spoon and run the relay race. You can use obstacles to make the race harder. Then, they have to run the race back to home base and give the spoon and egg (ping pong balls) to the next player in the line. If a student drops his egg or ball, he has to go back to the beginning. For younger students, the student can pick up the egg (ping pong ball) and continue from where he dropped it. Students can't use their other hands to touch, hold, or steady the egg (ping pong ball).

The team that has all the players run the race first wins.

Memory Verse Skit: (use Worship Power Lesson 1, slide A)

Supplies needed: doctor puppet or doctor costume for skit

Doctor Word: Hi kids. I'm Doctor Word. I'm called that because I'm a doctor and because I love the Word of God. The heart is only about the size of a fist, but it's a very important tool in the human body. The purpose of the heart is to pump blood through the network of blood vessels called the arteries and veins. This blood carries nutrients and oxygen throughout the body. If the heart stops beating, the nutrients and oxygen have no way to get to the other parts of the body, and the person dies.

Everyone of us was created for a purpose. That purpose is to worship God. If we don't carry out our purpose, our spiritual life suffers and eventually dies. That's why today's memory verse is so important. Luke 4:8b (NIV) says ...*Worship the Lord your God. He is the only one you should serve.*

Remember, worship is as important to your spiritual life as your heart is to your body. Worship is powerful.

Offering: Worship in Giving

(Mark 12:41-44)

Did you know offering is an act of worship? In the book of Mark, Jesus watched people giving their offering. Some rich people gave a lot in the offering, but a poor widow only gave a little bit. That's because she gave everything she had. Jesus told the disciples that she'd given the most because she gave everything. She loved God, and so she worshipped God by giving all she had.

Skit: Tyler the Power Tool Guy and His Power Tools

Supplies Needed: Tyler has a portable toolbox or toolbelt with various tools and is dressed in blue jeans and a plaid shirt, etc., a variety of power tools (If you don't have power tools, manual tools will do.) If you use a girl in the skit, have her dress the same and call her Tyler the Power Tool Gal.

(Tyler, the Power Tool Guy, comes into the room. All his tools are laid out on a table in the front.)

Leader: Tyler, the Power Tool Guy. I'm so glad you could come today.

Tyler the Power Tool Guy: You said you needed me. What happened? Do you have an outlet that needs replaced? Or maybe you had the roof collapse, and you need it fixed? That would be dangerous, you know. Or did you need me to build something? I have a lot of power tools. Just let me know what you need, and I'll build it for you.

Leader: Thanks, Tyler. I knew you'd want to help me, but I don't need anything built, fixed, or replaced.

Tyler: I don't understand. Why did you ask me to bring all my tools?

Leader: Today, we're teaching the children they were created to worship God. Everyone and everything have a purpose. I was wondering if you could explain the purpose of some of your tools.

Tyler: I'd love to. (Adlib here. Have Tyler show the student each tool on the table and tell what its purpose is.)

Leader: Thanks, Tyler. I appreciate you telling the children the purpose for each of these tools.

Tyler: No problem. I'm glad to do it. But there's something I don't understand.

Leader: What's that, Tyler.

Tyler: You said that the main purpose we were created for is to worship God. I thought my purpose in life was to repair things and to tell people about Jesus.

Leader: I have a couple of questions for you. Why do you tell others about Jesus? And why do you repair things?

Tyler: Those questions are easy. I tell other about Jesus because I love Him and I want people to know how wonderful He is. I repair things because God gave me an ability to do that, and I want to honor Him by doing a good job.

Leader: So, you love God, and because of that you tell others about Him and honor Him by doing the things He's called you to do?

Tyler: That's right.

Leader: In other words, you honor and worship God by telling other about Him and by repairing things.

Tyler: How about that? You're absolutely right. When I do the things God wants me to do, it's because I love Him and want to worship and honor Him.

Leader: See, Tyler. Your main purpose in life is to worship God. When you do that, everything else you do is to honor and serve Him. You were created to worship.

(Tyler exits)

Verse of the Day: Luke 4:8 (NIV) ...*Worship the Lord your God. He is the only one you should serve.*

Memory Verse Talk: (use Worship Power Lesson 1, slide A)

Have your students repeat the memory verse several times. *We were all created to worship God, but did you know that every person, whether he loves God or rejects Jesus as his Savior will worship Jesus. Even Satan will worship Jesus one day. Philippians 2:9-11 (NIV) says, "Therefore God exalted him to the highest place and gave him the name that is above every name, that at the name of Jesus every knee should bow, in heaven and on earth and under the earth, and every tongue acknowledge that Jesus Christ is Lord, to the glory of God the Father.*

We have a choice for now. We can worship Jesus and receive great satisfaction in doing what we were created to do, or we can refuse. But those who choose not to worship Jesus will one day have no choice. They will have to bow their knees and worship Him, but they won't getting any blessing or satisfaction from doing so.

I want to worship Jesus now, knowing that when I worship Him, I'm doing what I was created to do.

Memory Verse Activity: Memory Verse Chairs

Supplies needed: marker board, chalk board, or blank wall; scotch tape, colored sheets of paper (each sheet has one word of the memory verse on it)

Preparation: Tape the sheets of paper on the bottom of random chair the students will be sitting on.

Let the students know, the words of the memory verse are taped to their chairs. When you say go, the students will look under their seats and find the words. Then they tape them to the marker board or wall in order.

If you have enough students, have teams with different colors and make one set of words in each color.

Bible Story: Mary's Act of Worship

(John 12:1-8)

Supplies needed: perfume or spikenard essential oil

This is perfume (spikenard). Expensive perfume can cost a lot of money, but it sure smell good.

Spray perfume or dab on some spikenard so your students can smell it.

The most expensive perfume in the world is called Shumukh by Spirit of Dubai. It costs $1.295 million an ounce. I bet that perfume really smells good.

Good perfume has always been expensive. In Bible days, young women who could afford it would buy expensive perfume in an alabaster box made of marble. The only way to open the box to allow the scent of the perfume out was to break it. A woman would save the perfume box and break it on her wedding night so her husband could share the scent of the perfume with her.

This story is about a young woman named Mary who had an alabaster box of spikenard, an expensive perfume for that day. Her brother, Lazarus, had invited Jesus over for dinner. Mary loved her brother, Lazarus, and her sister, Martha. Earlier that week, Lazarus had died. Mary cried a lot when that happened, but Jesus brought Lazarus back to life. Mary was so grateful. She knew Jesus is the Son of God, and as much as she loved her brother and sister, she loved Jesus even more. She wanted to worship Him and show Him how much she loved Him.

Lazarus invited Jesus to his home, and Martha was cooking and serving dinner. Mary wanted to do something special for Jesus too. At some point, she remembered her alabaster box of spikenard perfume. No doubt, she had spent a lot of money on that perfume and was saving it for her wedding. That was the best way she could think of to worship Jesus.

She broke the alabaster box and poured it on Jesus' feet. Then she wiped his feet with her long hair. The beautiful fragrance of spikenard filled the room. The worship Mary had poured out smelled so good.

But one of Jesus' disciples was indignant. He told Jesus that what Mary did, pouring out that expensive perfume, was wrong and wasteful. She could have at least sold the perfume and given the money to the poor. Mary must have felt awful when Judas said that. She was just trying to pour out her love and worship on Jesus. Maybe she should have sold the perfume. She could have shown Jesus her love by feeding the poor.

Jesus shouted at Judas, "Leave her alone. She has done a beautiful thing."

Mary was so happy to hear Jesus say that. He understood that all she wanted to do was worship Him. Even the perfume she poured out wasn't as valuable to her as Jesus was.

Mary poured out extravagant worship on Jesus. God wants us to do the same. He wants us to pour out extravagant worship every time we worship Jesus. It's what He created us to do. When we worship Him, we feel satisfied in a way nothing else can satisfy because we are doing what God wants us to do, we are giving God glory.

Worship Expression: Tehillah (Use Power Worship Lesson 1, slide B)

Tehillah is a word that means to praise God with singing. That's why we sing songs every service. It's one way to worship and praise God. Psalm 149:1 (NIV) says, "Praise the Lord. Sing to the Lord a new song, his praise in the assembly of his faithful people." We're about to sing some songs, but we're not singing because it's something we always do in church or even because we like singing. Singing songs to God is one way of worshipping Him. As we sing today, let's think about the words as we sing our songs to God.

Praise and Worship: Choose a couple of fast song and a slow song to lead children into praise and worship. It works well to talk to the children about what worship is and why it's important before you enter into this time. You can have a children's praise team, but until they understand leading praise and worship, have an adult leader or yourself be the worship leader.

Video: Why Worship

Use Worship Power downloadable video, Why Worship, for Power Tools downloadable resources.

Object Lessons:

3. The Purpose of a Cup

Supplies needed: cup, bottle or pitcher of water

Show the students your cup. *Why do you think this cup was created?* Allow students to answer. Pour water into the cup and drink out of it. *This cup was created to drink fluid out of. What are some other things we can use this cup for even though it wasn't created for those things?* Allow students to answer. If they have trouble, make suggestions.

The reason we can use this cup for other things is because of the shape of the cup. It's easy to use the cup to drink from because it's shaped to hold liquid, and that means it can be used for those other things as well.

We are created to worship God. Because God made us to worship, we can do other things. Different people have different talents and gifts. They can use those talents and gift to honor God. Sometimes we tell our friends about Jesus and invite Him to church. We do that because we love and worship God and want our friends to love God too. It is an expression of worship. Sometimes people like to learn about science, math, or history, or they like to read a lot. The more we learn about God's creation, the more we can worship Him for what He's created. Some people work at jobs where they make lots of money. They can use that money to give an offering to worship God.

Whatever we do, we can do it unto the Lord. In other words, we were created to worship God in everything we do and are. The reverse is also true.

Pick up the cup. *I can refuse to drink out of this cup. I can throw it in the trash, so nobody will ever drink out of it again. Or I can poke holes in it so even if I do fill it with water, the water will leak out. That still doesn't change the fact that it is a cup.*

I was created to worship God, but I can refuse to worship God. I can say I don't believe in God or that I do believe in Him, but I don't want to worship Him. The problem is I was still created to be a worshipper, and I still will worship, but I'll worship other things. The Bible calls those things idols. Idols aren't just weird statues people in Bible times used to worship. An idol is anything we worship instead of God.

We can worship God with our money, or we can worship our money. We can worship God with our gifts and talents, or we can worship our gifts and talents. We can learn more about the world we live in and worship God for creating it, or we can worship math or science or the other things we study. We can worship God by telling our friends about Him, or we can worship our friends by doing things with them that we shouldn't be doing. Even something as simple as baseball or video games can become an idol if we put it before God. We were created to worship God not idols.

4. God Lives in Our Worship (Use Worship Power Lesson 1, slide C)

Supplies needed: Lego block or toy house

God has promised He will always be with Him, and that's true. God is everywhere at the same time, so He is always with us. But sometimes, we sense God's presence. We may feel a strange warmth or peace. Sometimes adults will say, "God is here." Of course, God is everywhere, but they mean they sense His presence. Many times, this happens when we are focused on God, when we pray, or when we are reading or listening to God's Word. Sometimes it even happens when we aren't doing any of those things.

Then there are times when the Manifest Presence of God shows up. The word, manifest, in the Bible means to uncover or make apparent. When we talk about the Manifest Presence of God, we're talking about uncovering and making apparent the Glory of God. When God's Glory is uncovered, a lot of things might happen. The Bible talks about people falling to the ground because they couldn't stand in the presence of God. This is sometimes called being slain in the Spirit.

In the book of Acts, the Bible describes people being so filled with the Holy Spirit and with joy and laughter, they appear drunk. Sometimes people fall on their knees or faces or take their shoes off. Sometimes they shout, and sing, and dance before the Lord. Sometimes people get very quiet. All of those things are the result of the Manifest Presence of God, but I'm going to talk about something that brings about the Manifest presence of God.

Show and read slide C. *Psalm 22:3 says, "But You are holy, enthroned in the praises of Israel." This verse says God is enthroned in the praise of His people. God sits on His throne in Heaven. Another word for His throne is His dwelling place or His house.*

Show Lego house. *When we worship God, God lives in our worship. His throne sits in our worship. That's why so many amazing things happen when we really decide to worship God with everything within us. Our worship is where God's glory lives. When we worship Him, He shows up and reveals Himself or uncovers Himself to us. Wow, no nonder worshipping God satisfies us like nothing else can.*

Message: Our Worship Shows Our Love (Use Power Worship Lesson 1, slide D)

Supplies Needed: none

Show slide D. One reason worship is so important to God is because it is the way we show God how much we love Him. In Matthew 22:37, "Jesus replied, 'Love the Lord your God with all your heart and with all your soul and with all your mind.'"

Someday, when you grow up, you might find someone you want to marry and spend the rest of your life with. When that happens, you'll want to express your love for that person. You might want to buy that person gifts or show affection by kissing or hugging. There are lots of ways to express love to the person you marry.

There are also lots of ways to express our love for God. We'll be learning more about these expressions of worship over the next few weeks. We've already learned how we can express our love to God by singing. I'm going to tell you a few other ways, and I want you all to act out the ways I tell you.

Have the children do each of these actions: kneeling, lying on the floor face up or face down, shouting hallelujah or Jesus, raising your hands, being very silent, spinning around, dancing.

Response Time:

Talk to the students about expressing their worship for God using one of these ways. Explain that you will play music and then lay your hand on each of their heads while they are worshipping. They should continue to worship while you're doing this and after you stop. Make sure you have a catcher for any students who might not be able to stand during worship.

Because God loves it when we express out love, He lives in our worship and makes us satisfied and joyful in Him. Some things might happen. You might feel so woozy you can't stand up. If that happens, our helper will stand behind you and gently lower you to the floor. Some of you might cry, but they will be tears that make you feel better. Some might laugh because God makes you so happy. Some of you might just stand, kneel, or sit while God fills you with His peace and love.

Whatever way, God shows Himself to you, don't rush it. Keep worshipping Him and staying in His manifest presence.

During response time, allow the Holy Spirit to lead you. Lay hands on the students as you see them respond to the Holy Spirit. Don't worry about saying the right thing or praying a long prayer. You can say simple phrases like "fill" or "more Lord." Keep your hand gently on each student's head until you feel led to go to the next student.

Small Group Activity: Debrief

Supplies needed: none

Spend some time talking to your students about what happened during worship time. Tell them about some of your past experiences worshipping God.

Lesson 2 - Worthy of Worship

Focus Point: We worship God because He is worthy of worship.

Goal: Students will learn that only God is worthy of our worship.

Verse of the Day: Psalm 29:2 (NKJV) *Give unto the Lord the glory due to His name; Worship the Lord in the beauty of holiness.*

Supplies Needed:

- doctor puppet or doctor costume for skit
- portable toolbox with various tools
- Tyler the Power Tool Guy Skit: Tyler wears a portable toolbox or toolbelt with various tools and is dressed in blue jeans and a plaid shirt, etc.
- toys, candy, and prizes
- story bag or tote bag
- stuffed animal sheep
- plant or picture of a bush
- flash paper (optional)
- lighter
- fake chains or picture of slave in chains
- name tag with I AM written on it
- name tag with YAHWEH written on it
- slice of bread
- flashlight
- Lego block door
- jar or glass
- pebbles
- sand
- pitcher of water

Opening: *Power Tools Countdown* (optional) or *Power Tools* Slide

Welcome: Worthy of Worship

Welcome children. Only God is worthy of worship, so let's start today's service with some praise and worship. For five minutes, let's tell God how worthy He is. You can shout Hallelujah or say you're worthy, or even I love you, Jesus.

Tell the students when to start. If your students are not ready for five minutes, start them out at one minute, and build from there.

Prayer: Ask a child to pray over the service.

Rules: (use rules slide) Go over the 5 Ups Rules.

Go over the *5 Ups Rules*: 1. Sit up straight. 2. Listen up. 3. Hush up. 4. Don't get up and run around or go to the bathroom. 5. Worship Up! (stand up and participate during praise and worship)

Theme or Activity Songs: Choose one of two fast moving activity or theme songs that go with the curriculum.

Game Time: Treasure Hunt (use game time slide)

Supplies needed: toys, candy, and prizes hidden around the room

Tell the students there are treasures hidden in the room. Let them know if there are any places they can't look. When you say go, they have five minutes to find all the prizes. You can let them know how many are hidden if you want. When the time is up, it's nice to have some extra small prizes for students who haven't found any.

As hard as you looked for some of these prizes, God is an even greater treasure we can seek by worshipping Him. Matthew 13:44 (NIV) says, "The kingdom of heaven is like treasure hidden in a field. When a man found it, he hid it again, and then in his joy went and sold all he had and bought that field."

Memory Verse Skit: (use Worship Power Lesson 2, slide A)

Supplies needed: doctor puppet or doctor costume for skit

Doctor Word: Hi kids. I'm Doctor Word. To become a doctor, I had to go to school for eight years. Then I took a difficult test to prove I knew everything I needed to know about medicine. You would think after all that, I would be a full-fledged doctor, but I had to become a resident and learn a specialty for three years. Some specialties take as long as six years. All the time and work was worth it because I became worthy to be called a doctor and a surgeon. Just think about it. God is the only being worthy of our praise and worship, not because He went to God school, but because He is that great. Psalm 29:2 (NKJV) *Give unto the Lord the glory due to His name; Worship the Lord in the beauty of holiness.* I love God so much that I show Him that love by worshipping Him.

Offering: Treasures in Heaven (use Worship Power Lesson 2, slide B)

Sometimes people call our money and possessions treasures. They call them that because they are valuable. God doesn't mind us having money and possessions, but He wants us to consider Him the most valuable thing in our lives. When we do that, we'll want to give in the offering to build the Kingdom of God.

Show slide B. *Matthew 6:21 (NIV) says, "For where your treasure is, there your heart will be also."*

Have a child pray over the offering.

Skit: Tyler the Power Tool Guy's Favorite Power Tool (use Worship Power Lesson 2, slides C & D)

Supplies needed: Tyler has a portable toolbox or toolbelt with various tools and is dressed in blue jeans and a plaid shirt, etc. If you use a girl in the skit, have her dress the same and call her Tyler the Power Tool Gal.

Tyler the Power Tool Guy: Hi, everyone. What are you learning about today?

Leader: Hello, Tyler the Power Tool Guy. We're learning that only God is worthy of our worship. Remember how I asked you to show us your favorite power tool today?

Tyler: I sure do.

Leader: It must be pretty small. I don't see it anywhere.

Tyler: Nope, it's not small. It's big. I couldn't bring it because it's too big to carry. But I did bring a picture. (Show slide C)

Leader: That tool looks complicated to use. What is it?

Tyler: It's called a lathe. It is complicated, but it does so much. I use it for shaping and cutting designs in metal and wood. It shapes, drills, sands, knurls, turns, cuts, and forms. It's hard to learn to use, but once you learn, it is a great power tool.

Leader: Are you an expert at it?

Tyler: No, I wouldn't call myself an expert, but I do a lot on the lathe. I have a picture of something I created using this tool. (Show slide D) See the design in the chair? I did that with a lathe.

Leader: That's amazing. You have a lot of talent.

Tyler: Awe, shucks. It was nothing. I couldn't have done it without my lathe. I guess you could say my lathe is a little like God.

Leader: I don't understand. A lathe is a power tool, and God is... well... God.

Tyler: True, but a lathe is my only power tool worthy of being called my favorite tool, and God is the only one worthy of my worship.

Leader: Oh, now I see what you mean.

Tyler: I have to go now. I need to clean my lathe. Bye. (Tyler exits.)

Verse of the Day: Psalm 29:2 (NKJV) *Give unto the Lord the glory due to His name; Worship the Lord in the beauty of holiness.*

Memory Verse Talk: (use Worship Power Lesson 2, slide A)

I am so happy that God gives me the opportunity to worship Him. Psalm 29:2 (NKJV) says, "Give unto the Lord the glory due to His name; Worship the Lord in the beauty of holiness." According to this verse, I worship God because He is the only one who has glory due His name. Not only that, but God is holy, and His holiness is beauty. Nobody else is holy and has glory like my God.

Memory Verse Activity: (use Worship Power Lesson 2, slide A)

Supplies needed: none

Have your students sing this memory verse. You can teach them to sing the words to a song they already know, or you can use the song, **Give Unto the Lord the Glory** by Scriptures for Kids. It can be found at this YouTube link. https://www.youtube.com/watch?v=qPHFv_PbSik

Bible Story: Moses Learns God's Name & Jesus Uses God's Name

(Exodus 3:1-15)

Supplies needed: story bag or tote bag with stuffed animal sheep, plant or picture of a bush, flash paper (optional), lighter, fake chains or picture of slave in chains, name tag with I AM written on it, name tag with YAHWEH written on it, slice of bread, flashlight, Lego block door

Preparation: Place items in a tote bag or story bag and pull them out as you're telling the story.

Did you know God has a name? A lot of people think that God's name is God, but that isn't true. He is God, but that's not His name. Some people say God's name is Jesus. That is true. God the Son is named Jesus, and His name is Holy, but God the Father isn't Jesus, and God the Holy Spirit isn't Jesus. There is one name God has that God the Father, God the Son, and God the Holy Spirit share. That's the name that has God's glory attached to it. Would you like to know what that name is? Then listen to these stories.

Show stuffed sheep. *The first story happened when Moses was tending sheep. Moses saw a bush on fire in a nearby cave.*

Show plant or picture of a bush. *The unusual thing about this bush was even though it was on fire, it didn't burn up the bush. This wasn't an ordinary fire. God was in that bush, and He is sometimes called a consuming fire.* Light flash paper (optional) or lighter.

God called out to Moses, and Moses went in the cave to get a closer look. Not only was God in the burning bush but He spoke to Moses. He told Moses to take off His shoes because this is a holy place. Show shoes or sandals. *The truth is anywhere God shows up in His glory is a holy place because God is holy.*

Moses knew that, and He hid His face because He was in awe of the beauty of God's holiness. God told him that He wanted him to go to Egypt to rescue God's people from slavery. Show fake chains or picture of slave in chains.

Moses was surprised because he didn't believe he was worthy of carrying out a mission like this, but God told him to go. He asked God who he should tell them sent him. That's when God told Moses His name. He said, I AM is sending you. Show name badge with I AM written on it.

Many of the names God uses begins with I AM. In the Hebrew language, I AM is YAHWEH, the most Holy name of God. Show name tag with YAHWEH written on it.

I AM means He is always with us. I am means He is everything we need. What we want or need God to be, He is I AM. That's a great reason to worship Him.

When Jesus came to Earth, because He is God, He used the name Jesus, but He also used the name I AM. He said, "I AM the bread of light." Show bread.

I AM the light of the world. Show flashlight.

He said, "I AM the door." Show a Lego block door.

And He said, "I AM the Way, the Truth, and the Life. Those are amazing statements. They mean that Jesus is the Holy God. In John 8:58, Jesus said, "Very truly I tell you," Jesus answered, "before Abraham was born, I AM!" So when we are worshipping Jesus, we are worshipping God.

Optional Video: That's My King

This would be a great time to show the video ***That's My King***. Your church may already own it. You can find it at Worship House or on YouTube at this link. https://youtu.be/yzqTFNfeDnE

Worship Expression: Barak (Use Worship Power Lesson 2, slide E)

The word Barak means to bow down before God. A lot of people think this means they're supposed to kneel before they pray, but it means much more. In Heaven, when Christians see Jesus, they will bow at His feet and give any rewards they've been given to Him. In Revelation 4:11, they'll say, "You are worthy, our Lord and God to receive glory and honor and power, for you created all things, and by your will they were created and have their being." It also says that at the name of Jesus, every knee shall bow. So, when we worship and behold the glory and beauty of God, we won't bow because we've been told we should. We'll bow because God is worthy of our worship.

Praise and Worship: Choose a couple of fast song and a slow song to lead children into praise and worship. It works well to talk to the children about what worship is and why it's important before you enter into this time. You can have a children's praise team, but until they understand leading praise and worship, have an adult leader or yourself be the worship leader.

Object Lesson:

3. Object Lesson: Wow Moments

Supplies needed: none

Have you ever had a wow moment? I have.

Tell about a time or something you saw that made you go wow. It could be seeing the Grand Canyon, Niagara Falls or a double rainbow, or your wedding day, or when you first saw your child. Allow some of your students to tell about some of their wow moments.

We've all had wow moments in our lives, and hopefully we'll have many more. But when we worship God, and He shows us His glory, that's a wow moment bigger than any other wow moment could ever be. Even the names God uses make us go wow.

Adonai means the Lord God.

Yahweh means the Great I Am.

El Shaddai means God Almighty.

El Roi means the God who sees me.

Elohim is Father God or God the Creator of everything.

Yahweh Yireh means I AM your Provider.

Yahweh Ropheka means I AM your Healer.

Yahweh Nissi I AM your banner.

Yahweh Shalom means I AM your Peace.

Yahweh Tsuri means I AM your Rock.

El Olam means The Eternal God.

Yeshua means Jesus, the Son of God.

Can we all say Wow together? Wow.

4. Object Lesson: Magnify the Lord

Supplies needed: magnifying glass or binoculars

Allow each student to look through the magnifying glass.

What happens when you look through this magnifying glass (binoculars). Allow the students to answer.

In a way, worship works in the same way. God appears bigger when we worship Him. That's why King David said in Psalm 34:3 (NKJV), "Oh, magnify the Lord with me, And let us exalt His name together." King David wanted to worship God and His Name, so God would appear bigger to him.

When we looked at the objects through the magnifying glass (binoculars), all the items appeared bigger. Were they really bigger? Allow the students to answer.

That's the difference between worship and a magnifier. God is bigger and more spectacular than we could ever understand or know. When we worship, He appears bigger to us, but He is much bigger and greater than He ever appears to us.

Message: Spiritual Act of Worship (Use Worship Power Lesson 2, slide F)

Supplies needed: jar or glass, pebbles, sand, pitcher of water

Show slide E. *Romans 12:1 says, "Therefore, I urge you, brothers and sisters, in view of God's mercy, to offer your bodies as a living sacrifice, holy and pleasing to God—this is your true and proper worship."*

This isn't just a one-time thing where we get saved and give our lives to God. God wants us to continually give more of our lives to Him. It's a lifetime act of worship.

Show jar. *This jar represents giving our lives to God. Is this jar full?* Allow students to answer. If nobody mentions it, point out that the jar is full of air. *We give our lives to God when we get saved, but there's so much more we can give than just air.*

Pour pebbles into the jar. *We can go to church and read our Bible. We can tell God we love Him, and begin to worship Him in church. Now, is the jar full? It's full, but there's still more we can give.*

Pour sand into the jar. *We can start living our lives for God. We can tell our friends about Jesus and show love to others. Is the jar full now? There's still more we can give.*

Pour water into the jar. *When we sacrifice our lives to God, there's always more we can give to Him, but everything we give in worship is rewarded with a satisfying life. Is the jar full now?* Allow students to answer.

Yes, the jar is full, but there's still more. If you took a microscope and looked at the molecules in this jar, you would see there's still more room. There's always more of our lives we can give.

Response Time and Worship Expression: Barak (Use Worship Power Lesson 2, slide F)

The word Barak means to bow down before God. A lot of people think this means they're supposed to kneel before they pray, but it means much more. In Heaven, when Christians see Jesus, they will bow at His feet and give any rewards they've been given to Him. We will give Him everything. In Revelation 4:11, they'll say, "You are worthy, our Lord and God to receive glory and honor and power, for you created all things, and by your will they were created and have their being." It also says that at the name of Jesus, every knee shall bow. So, when we worship and behold the glory and beauty of God, we won't bow because we've been told we should. We'll bow because God is worthy of our worship.

Let's take some time to worship. If you want to bow down you can. Let the students know you will be laying a hand on their heads and praying for them like you did last week. This time, pray they give more of themselves in worship.

Small Group Activity: Worship Expression Zamar

Supplies needed: kid's instruments (You can make these from common household items if the church doesn't have kid's instruments. Check online for how to make them. If you have time, you might even allow the students to make the instruments.)

Zamar means to worship God joyfully with musical instruments, so we're going to take some time to play these instruments. You don't have to play them well, but I'd like you to play them joyfully.

Lesson 3 - Worship In Spirit and In Truth

Focus Point: God wants us to worship in spirit and in truth.

Goal: Students will learn what it means to worship Him in spirit and in truth.

Verse of the Day: John 4:24 (NKJV) *God is Spirit, and those who worship Him must worship in spirit and truth.*

Supplies Needed:

- doctor puppet or doctor costume for skit
- portable toolbox with various tools
- Tyler the Power Tool Guy Skit: Tyler wears a portable toolbox or toolbelt with various tools and is dressed in blue jeans and a plaid shirt, etc.
- engraved wood project (optional)
- bouncing ball
- bottle of water
- pitcher of water
- lotta bowl (optional object you can find online or in a magic shop)
- cup
- Styrofoam cup with holes punch in the bottom
- bowl or tray
- small table
- a few unbreakable items to set on table

Opening: *Power Tools Countdown* (optional) or *Power Tools* Slide

Welcome:

Welcome children. God wants us to worship Him in spirit and in truth. We'll learn what that means today, but let's start this service with some praise and worship. For five minutes, let's tell worship God and tell Him how worthy He is. You can shout Hallelujah or say you're worthy, or even I love you, Jesus.

Tell the students when to start. If your students are not ready for five minutes, start them out at one minute, and build from there.

Prayer: Ask a child to pray over the service.

Rules: (use rules slide) Go over the 5 Ups Rules.

Go over the *5 Ups Rules*: 1. Sit up straight. 2. Listen up. 3. Hush up. 4. Don't get up and run around or go to the bathroom. 5. Worship Up! (stand up and participate during praise and worship)

Theme or Activity Songs: Choose one of two fast moving activity or theme songs that go with the curriculum.

Game Time: Jesus Says Worship (use game time slide)

Supplies needed: none

This is played the same way as Simon Says, only you say Jesus says. Say various things children might do to worship God. Some suggestions are stomp your feet, jump up and down, sing, kneel, clap your hands, raise your hands, lay on the floor, spin around, dance, etc.

Memory Verse Skit: (use Worship Power Lesson 3, slide A)

Supplies needed: doctor puppet or doctor costume for skit

Doctor Word: Hi kids. I'm Doctor Word. I'm called that because I'm a doctor and because I love the Word of God. There are certain procedures I must follow as a doctor licensed by the state. For instance, I can't tell anyone about a patient's health unless that patient gives me permission. And there are certain drugs I can only prescribe if I document why the patient needs them. When I perform surgery, there are policies for making sure I have a sterile surgical room. I also must wash my hands a certain way and wear gloves, a mask, a hair cover, and a surgical gown. There are good reasons for each of these policies, and I always make sure I follow them. To not do so could end in disaster for the patient and for me.

There are also policies you should follow to worship God. Some people think those policies include how you worship. Do you raise your hands or fall down? Do you laugh or cry? Do you shout or be very quiet? But God doesn't care how you worship. All of those ways to worship are pleasing to Him if you follow His worship policy. It's easy to remember because it's our memory verse for today. John 4:24 (NKJV) says, *"God is Spirit, and those who worship Him must worship in spirit and truth."* The spirit part means we worship from our whole heart and surrender to what the Holy Spirit wants to do. The truth part means we always worship according to Scripture. We never try to worship doing something that Scripture tells us not to do. For instance, we would never use icons or special crystals to help us worship. I have to go now. Remember to worship in spirit and in truth.

Offering: Giving to Be Blessed

Giving is an act of worship. Just like in worship, when we give with our heart out of love for God, God will bless us and be pleased with our offering, but if we give because we have to, that doesn't honor God or make Him happy with our giving. We want to give in the right way, as an act of worship. That's when it's more blessed to give than to receive.

Skit: Tyler the Power Tool Guy Makes a Project

Supplies Needed: Tyler has a portable toolbox or toolbelt with various tools and is dressed in blue jeans and a plaid shirt, etc. If you use a girl in the skit, have her dress the same and call her Tyler the Power Tool Gal. If you have a woodworker in your church, use one of his creations as an object lesson. Change the script accordingly. If not, use Worship Power Lesson 3, slide B.

Tyler the Power Tool Guy: Hi there. Today, I wanted to show you something I made with my lathe power tool. I'm very proud of it.

Leader: I'd love to see it.

Tyler: It's still at my woodshop, but I have a picture of it.

(Show slide B)

Leader: That's beautiful. What is it?

Tyler: It's the lid for a chest I'm making. I'm pretty proud of it.

Leader: That's amazing. Did you do all of that engraving with your lathe?

Tyler: Not all of it. I used a power saw and a jigsaw for parts of it, and I had to hand carve to more delicate parts, but without my lathe, it would have taken a lot longer to make.

Leader: It's obvious you put a lot of time and effort into making this.

Tyler: I did. It's a gift for someone very special. I wanted to let this person know how much I care.

Leader: That's a little bit like what I'm teaching about today..

Tyler: I don't understand. Your teaching about woodworking in church?

Leader: No, not that. I'm teaching about worshipping God in spirit and in truth. Worship is expressing our love for God. You are expressing your love for this special person in your woodworking. Just as we should express our worship in spirit and in truth, your expressing yourself with you skill and passion.

Tyler: Don't forget my power tools.

Leader: That's right. And your power tools.

Tyler: That makes a lot of sense, but I need to go put the finishing touches on this chest lid now. Good-bye.

(Exits)

Verse of the Day: John 4:24 (NKJV) *God is Spirit, and those who worship Him must worship in spirit and truth.*

Memory Verse Talk: (use Worship Power Lesson 3, slide A)

Supplies needed: None

John 4:24 (NKJV) says, "God is Spirit, and those who worship Him must worship in spirit and truth." Worship isn't about what we see on the outside. While people who are worshipping God might jump up and down, shout, sing, cry, and laugh, that isn't worship. If we are truly worshipping, that's only the expressions of our worship. True worship happens in the heart. When we surrender our lives to the Holy Spirit and we trust His Word, the Bible, then we are worshipping in spirit and in truth.

Memory Verse Activity: Bouncing Ball

Supplies needed: bouncing ball

Have your students stand in a circle. When the ball is bounced to a student, that student must say the next word in the verse. Repeat several times until everyone has had a turn.

Bible Story: The Woman at the Well

(John 4:4-26)

Supplies needed: bottle of water, Worship Power Lesson 3, slides B through D

I'm really thirsty. I've been thirsty all morning. Excuse me while I have a drink of water. Drink water from the water bottle and tell your students how it really quenched your thirsty.

Today, I'm going to tell you the story of a time when Jesus was thirsty. He was in a place called Samaria, and He sat down at a well.

Show slide B. *Now, we go to the store and buy water bottles to take with us on long walks, but back then, they didn't have water bottles. When you were thirsty, you had to find a well and lower a pail or a cup into the well to get some water. I'm glad we don't have to do that every time we want to take a long walk.*

Jesus sat at the well around noon, the hottest time of day. He was so thirsty, but he didn't have a cup or a pail to lower into the well. I bet you were thinking, "Why doesn't he just invent a water bottle or created a cup out of thin air." He could have done that. He could have even made a wooden cup since He was a carpenter, but Jesus had other plans.

Show slide C. *Just then, a woman walked up to the well carrying water jugs. She wasn't just any woman. She was a Samaritan woman. Jews in those days thought Samaritans weren't even worthy of talking to, but Jesus doesn't have any prejudices like that. He created everyone to be of equal worth. He spoke to the Samaritan woman and asked her for a drink of water. The Samaritan woman was surprised that a Jew would talk to her, let alone ask her for a drink. Jews just didn't do that.*

When the Samaritan woman asked why He asked her for a drink, Jesus told her if she knew who He was, she would ask Him for a drink. Then He said that He had living water. Whoever drank from the water He had would never thirst again. She didn't know this, but Jesus was talking about the living water God gives us when we get saved. It satisfies our soul like nothing can. Jesus surprised her again and told her about her life and the wrong things she'd done. He was letting her know that the life she was living away from God would never satisfy her.

The woman knew Jesus must be special. She believed He was a prophet, but she was confused about worship and wanted to know where people should worship. The Samaritans worshipped on a mountain, and the Jews worshipped in the temple in Jerusalem.

Jesus told her it didn't matter where she worshipped. The important thing was how she worshipped.

Show slide D. *In John 4: 23-24 (NKJV), Jesus said, "Yet a time is coming and has now come when the true worshipers will worship the Father in the Spirit and in truth, for they are the kind of worshipers the Father seeks. God is spirit, and his worshipers must worship in the Spirit and in truth."*

God doesn't care where we worship or how we express our worship. God cares about what is in our hearts. He wants us to worship Him in Spirit and in Truth.

Worship Expression: Yadah (Use Worship Power Lesson 3, slides E & F)

Show slide E. *Our praise word for today is Yadah. It means to raise our hand to God. It is a sign of surrender and adoration.*

Show slide F. *The word is used in Psalm 63:1-4. "You, God, are my God, earnestly I seek you; I thirst for you, my whole being longs for you, in a dry and parched land where there is no water. I have seen you in the sanctuary and beheld your power and your glory. Because your love is better than life, my lips will glorify you. I will praise you as long as I live, and in your name I will YADAH lift up my hands."*

So let's Yadah today as we worship.

Praise and Worship: Choose a couple of fast song and a slow song to lead children into praise and worship. It works well to talk to the children about what worship is and why it's important before you enter into this time. You can have a children's praise team, but until they understand leading praise and worship, have an adult leader or yourself be the worship leader.

Object Lessons:

3. Living Water and Broken Wells

Supplies needed: pitcher of water, lotta bowl (optional object you can find online or in a magic shop), cup, Styrofoam cup with holes punch in the bottom, bowl or tray to catch excess water

As you are reading the following paragraph to your students, fill a cup with water until it overflows. If you are using a lotta bowl, have it filled completely before the service, and pour out water from time to time throughout the lesson saying, *God's living water never runs dry.* The lotta bowl will appear as if it has an endless supply of water.

In Jeremiah 2:13, God corrected His people for committing two sins. The first was forsaking God who He called the spring of living water, and the second was going to broken wells that couldn't hold any water. I have here a pitcher of water (lotta bowl). When we love and worship God. He fills us to overflowing. We never run out of His living water. The Holy Spirit fills us and satisfies us with His joy and peace like springs of living water.

As you read the next paragraph, pour water into the Styrofoam cup. It should leak our of the holes you've punched in the bottom.

But God also said that His people were using broken wells that hold no water. That is what happens when your worship is just a duty you feel like you have to do and you don't worship in spirit and in truth. Anything you love more than God becomes like a broken well. It can never satisfy your thirst. There are lots of things we can do that aren't a sin, but if we put them before God, they become like broken wells. Can you name a few things people put before God? Allow the students to answer.

How do we get this living water? Jesus is the living water. In John 7:38 (NIV), Jesus says, "Whoever believes in me, as Scripture has said, rivers of living water will flow from within them."

4. Vain Worship

(Matthew 21:12-13; Mark 11:15-18)

Supplies needed: small table with unbreakable items.

Knock over the table. Let the students know you did this to show an object lesson and not because you were angry. Ask them if they were surprised you did that. Ask them how they would feel if Jesus came into church next week and knock over the tables.

This happened in the Bible. The worship in the temple was so displeasing to God that Jesus went into the temple, knocked over the tables, and drove people out with a whip. Wow. He must have been really angry. He told them why He was so angry about their worship. Here are two kinds of worship God doesn't like.

Hypocritical Worship: Jesus doesn't like worship that is only lip service. If you pretend to worship God with your words, but you don't love God, it isn't true worship. God wants us to worship from the heart. This is worshipping with our spirit. Mark 7:6.

False Worship: Jesus told the people they were following a bunch of rules about worshipping God that weren't even in the Bible. When you try to worship, but you don't believe what the Bible says, it is false worship. God wants us to know Him by studying His Word. Then we will worship Him in truth. Matthew 15:9.

God is pleased with our worship when we worship Him in Spirit and in truth.

Message: The Kind of Worship that Pleases God

Supplies needed: none

Just as there are kind of worship that God hates, there is worship that pleases God.

Worship in spirit and in truth. We know about this worship from our memory verse and Bible story. John 4:24 (NKJV) God is Spirit, and those who worship Him must worship in spirit and truth.

Worship from a pure heart and clean hands. Psalm 24:3-4 (NIV) Who may ascend the mountain of the Lord? Who may stand in his holy place? The one who has clean hands and a pure heart, who does not trust in an idol or swear by a false god. To have a pure heart, we accept Jesus as our Savior. To have clean hands, we do what's right and ask God to forgive us when we fail.

Worship in faith. Hebrews 11:6 (NIV) says, "And without faith it is impossible to please God, because anyone who comes to him must believe that he exists and that he rewards those who earnestly seek him." When we believe in God, seek Him, and know He will reward us with His joy and peace, then we worship the way God wants.

Worship Expression and Response Time: Hallal (Use Worship Power Lesson 3, slide G & H)

The word, Hallal, is the main word for praise. It's the word that makes the word hallelujah. It means to be clear, to praise, to shine, to boast, show, to rave, celebrate, to be clamorously foolish. In other words, it means to joyfully celebrate God.

Show slide G. *HALLAL is a primary Hebrew root word for praise. Our word "hallelujah" comes from this base word. It's used in Psalm 150. I want you all to repeat the words in a joyful way to celebrate the Lord. You can even shout the words if you want.*

Show Slide H. *Psalm 150 Praise the Lord. Praise God in his sanctuary; praise him in his mighty heavens.*

Praise him for his acts of power; praise him for his surpassing greatness.

Praise him with the sounding of the trumpet, praise him with the harp and lyre,

Praise him with timbrel and dancing, praise him with the strings and pipe,

Praise him with the clash of cymbals, praise him with resounding cymbals.

Let everything that has breath praise the Lord. Praise the Lord.

Have the students spend some time celebrating and worshipping God. Let the students know you will be laying a hand on their heads and praying for them like you did last week. After worship time, ask them what happened or what they felt during worship time.

Small Group Activity and Worship Expression: Praise Ye the Lord

Supplies needed: none

This is a classic children's ministry song. If you've never heard it, you can find it on YouTube at this link. https://www.youtube.com/watch?v=p8OylXvM384 The music is a bit dorky, so I recommend you don't use it unless you find a more modernized version. Divide the students into two teams. One team sings Hallelu, Hallelujah. The other team sings Praise Ye the Lord. Then you can alternate. The loudest team wins.

Show slide L. *There is one more praise and worship word I want to teach you today. The word is Shabach. Shabach means to shout praises to God, so when we sing this next song, we're going to shout praises to God.* Instruct the students how to sing this game.

Lesson 4 - Enjoying Worship

Focus Point: Worship enjoying God.

Goal: Students will learn God wants them to enjoy Him through worship.

Verse of the Day: Psalm 16:11 (NKJV) *You will show me the path of life; In Your presence is fullness of joy. At Your right hand are pleasures forevermore.*

Supplies Needed:

- doctor puppet or doctor costume for skit
- portable toolbox with various tools
- Tyler the Power Tool Guy Skit: Tyler wears a portable toolbox or toolbelt with various tools and is dressed in blue jeans and a plaid shirt, etc.
- Snickers bar
- balloon filled halfway with water
- candle
- lighter
- bottle of bubbles

Opening: *Power Tools Countdown* (optional) or *Power Tools* Slide

Welcome: Prayer Time

Welcome. For the last three weeks, we've been learning about the power of worship. Today we're going to talk about how God wants us to have fun worshipping Him. For five minutes, let's enjoy God by worshipping Him. You can shout Hallelujah or say you're worthy, or even I love you, Jesus.

Tell the students when to start. If your students are not ready for five minutes, start them out at one minute, and build from there.

Prayer: Ask a child to pray over the service.

Rules: (use rules slide) Go over the 5 Ups Rules.

Go over the *5 Ups Rules*: 1. Sit up straight. 2. Listen up. 3. Hush up. 4. Don't get up and run around or go to the bathroom. 5. Worship Up! (stand up and participate during praise and worship)

Theme or Activity Songs: Choose one of two fast moving activity or theme songs that go with the curriculum.

Game Time: Dance Contest (use game time slide)

Supplies Needed: none

For this game, you can choose a certain number of students or have every student participate. If you have every student participate, choose someone to judge the contest. If only a certain number of students participate, then have the other students judge the contest by clapping for each student participating. The goal of the contest is to have each student dance to upbeat music. When the game ends, tell the students how King David danced before the Lord as an expression of worship.

Memory Verse Skit: (use Worship Power Lesson 4, slide A)

Supplies needed: doctor puppet or doctor costume for skit

Doctor Word: Hi kids. I'm Doctor Word. I'm called that because I'm a doctor and because I love the Word of God. I love being a doctor. Helping people get better when they are sick is a joy I can't describe. But it doesn't even compare to the joy that comes from worshipping God and being in His presence. Psalm 16:11 (NKJV) says, *"You will show me the path of life; In Your presence is fullness of joy; At Your right hand are pleasures forevermore."* Let's enjoy God today.

Offering: Joyful Giving

Did you know God wants us to be happy when we give in the offering? 2 Corinthians 9:6 (NKJV) says, "God loves a cheerful giver." So, let's all cheer before we give today. Encourage children to clap and shout, "Praise the Lord."

Skit: Tyler the Power Tool Guy

Supplies Needed: Tyler has a portable toolbox or toolbelt with various tools and is dressed in blue jeans and a plaid shirt, etc. If you use a girl in the skit, have her dress the same and call her Tyler the Power Tool Gal.

Tyler the Power Tool Guy: (Comes in) Hi everyone. I can't stay long today.

Leader: I'm sorry to hear that, Tyler. I was hoping you'd tell us some more about your lathe and wooden chest.

Tyler: I wish I could, but the boss had me working overtime so much this week that I didn't have time to work on my project.

Leader: Why so much overtime?

Tyler: We have a new job. Someone bought a fixer upper house and hired us to fix it up.

Leader: That sounds like fun.

Tyler: It can be, but I enjoy making things so much more than fixing something that's broken. That's sort of how I feel about this house. I like fixing it up, but I really enjoy making things like that chest. I have to go now. Bye, everyone.

(Exits)

Verse of the Day: Psalm 16:11 (NKJV) *You will show me the path of life; In Your presence is fullness of joy; At Your right hand are pleasures forevermore.*

Memory Verse Talk: (use Worship Power Lesson 4, slide A)

Supplies needed: none

Psalm 16:11 (NKJV) says, "You will show me the path of life; In Your presence is fullness of joy; At Your right hand are pleasures forevermore." Let's look at this verse for a moment. Jesus said, "I am the way, the truth, and the life," so God shows us the path of life, and that path is in Jesus. That should make us happy since all we have to do is give our lives to Him, and He'll guide us every step of the way.

We've been talking about worship the last few weeks and how worship brings us into the manifest presence of God. In God's presence is fullness of joy. At His right hand are pleasures forever.

Have you ever heard someone say they don't want to follow God because they want to have fun? Those people don't understand that we are the one's having fun. God wants to fill us up with His joy. Some Christians believe that they have to be sad and serious when they're worshipping God. I hope you realize by now that God wants to fill us with joy. He doesn't want us to be sad in His presence. He wants us to shout, and cheer, and laugh, and dance.

Memory Verse Activity: Say It with Motions

Divide the class into teams of four to six students each. Try to include a couple of older students in each team. The teams have five minutes to come up with motions to act out for the memory verse. Give each team a chance to show their motions.

Bible Story: David Danced

(2 Samuel 6:12-19)

Supplies Needed: none

Tell your students to listen to this story carefully. Whenever you say dance, they are to get up and leap, dance, or spin. Whenever you say sad, they are to cry boo hoo, boo hoo.

*Have you ever had something so exciting happen that you wanted to leap up and down, dance, and spin? When we are **happy**, we sometimes feel like doing just that. This story is about King David. King David was called a man after God's own heart. He was called that because, even though he made mistakes that made God **sad**, He loved to worship God. It made him **happy**.*

*(Show slide B) This is the Ark of the Covenant. In King David's time, it was how God showed His manifest presence and glory to His people. King David wanted the ark to be in Jerusalem, his capital city, so God's presence would always be close to him. He tried to move the ark once before, but he did it the wrong way, and it ended in tragedy. David left the ark in a tent miles away for the city. It made him **sad** the ark wasn't near him.*

*One day, David decided he would move the ark to his city. He studied God's Word to make sure He moved the ark the right way this time. As the men carried the ark into the city, David was so **happy**. He had musicians play, trumpets blast, and singers sing. Some people were so **happy** they started shouting praises to God. Before long, David became so **happy**, he removed his outer coat and danced before the Lord with all his might. This made God very **happy**.*

*With all the praises, worship, and dancing going on to worship the Lord, you would think it would make everyone **happy** that the Ark of the Covenant, God's presence, was coming into Jerusalem, but it didn't. David's wife was angry. She thought dancing, shouting, and singing before the Lord was undignified. This made David **sad** and angry. He told her he would become even more undignified worshipping God. Worshipping God made him **happy**, and he wasn't going to let anyone stop his worship.*

Worship Expression: Machowl (Use Worship Power Lesson 4, slide B)

Machowl means to worship God by dancing or spinning about. It's the way David expressed his worship to God when he danced. It's found in Psalm 149:3 (NIV). Let them praise his name with dancing and make music to him with timbrel and harp.

It's now time for praise and worship. Let's praise God today by spinning around or dancing. For praise and worship, choose songs the students can dance to.

Praise and Worship: Choose a couple of fast song and a slow song to lead children into praise and worship. It works well to talk to the children about what worship is and why it's important before you enter into this time. You can have a children's praise team, but until they understand leading praise and worship, have an adult leader or yourself be the worship leader.

Object Lessons:

3. God Satisfies

Supplies needed: Snickers bar

If you have snack time, consider serving Snickers bite size candy bars. Have an alternate for students allergic to nuts.

Snickers used to have an advertising slogan that said, "Snickers really satisfies you." While it's nice to think that a sugary chocolate candy bar can satisfy your hunger, it doesn't. What it really does is make you hungry for more sugary treats.

Worshipping God is not like a Snickers bar. God satisfies us like nothing can. Psalm 107:9 (NASB) says, "For He has satisfied the thirsty soul." When we worship and enjoy the Lord, He will satisfy us. Now, that's a slogan I can get behind.

4. Joy in the Flame

Supplies needed: balloon filled halfway with water, candle, lighter

Preparation: Fill the balloon halfway with water, and light the candle.

Today, we are talking about enjoying God in worship. Some people wonder how you can have the joy of the Lord, when things are going wrong. There may be a sickness in your family, or your parents might be fighting or getting a divorce. You might have had a fight with your best friend, or a bully might be picking on you at school. How can you have joy when things like that are happening?

There are many people in the Bible who went through hard times. Paul was imprisoned and beaten. Peter was thrown in prison more than once. And John was boiled in oil. When they couldn't kill John, they banished him to a remote island. Even so, none of these disciples lost their joy. That's because the joy of the Lord is a supernatural joy given by the Holy Spirit. It means God is larger than your problems, so you are satisfied in Him. When you worship, God gives you that kind of joy. The more you worship, the larger God becomes in your life. He gives you joy that can't be quenched by any flame of difficulty.

Show balloon and light candle. *Pretend this balloon is a Christian. He's been worshipping, and he has the joy of the Holy Spirit inside him. After he leaves church, he might have something bad happen to him.*

Place the balloon over the fire. Make sure you place the balloon so the part with water is touching the flames. You may want to practice this before the service.

Even though trials come, if we are worshipping and the Holy Spirit lives inside of us, the flames of those trials won't destroy us. It's all right to feel sad when bad things happen, but when we worship Jesus even though we are sad, it's possible to be joyful and sad at the same time.

Optional Video: Joy is Contagious

Sometimes it's easier for children to get this concept if they see it. Here are a few videos on YouTube you might want to show your students. These videos are long, so I suggest you only show a few minutes of one or two of them.

https://youtu.be/IBiwQhbyfkk

https://youtu.be/SyiqPQ4ZY6c

https://youtu.be/L88V4qAtUDU

Message: It's Bubbling (Use Worship Power Lesson 4, slide C, D, E)

Supplies needed: bottle of bubbles

Start making bubbles and continue throughout the object lesson. *I bet you wonder why I have this bottle of bubbles. I'm using these bubbles to illustrate how God wants to fill you with so much joy that it bubbles out of you.*

Romans 15:13 (NKJV) says, "Now may the God of hope fill you with all joy and peace in believing, that you may abound (bubble up) in hope by the power of the Holy Spirit."

John 4:14 (NKJV) says, "But whoever drinks of the water that I shall give him will never thirst. But the water that I shall give him will become in him a fountain of water springing (bubbling) up into everlasting life."

1 Peter 1:8 (NIV) says, "Though you have not seen him, you love him; and even though you do not see him now, you believe in him and are filled (bubbling up) with an inexpressible and glorious joy.

One thing all these verses show us is that when we are worshipping God, He wants to fill us with joy until it bubbles up inside. When joy fills you and bubbles us inside of you, sometimes it will cause you to smile, and sometimes it will even cause you to laugh. God loves us and wants us to enjoy worshipping Him.

Response Time:

For response time, have the students spend some time celebrating and worshipping God. Let the students know you will be laying a hand on their heads and praying for them to be filled with joy. Tell them to expect God to fill them with joy, and sometimes laughter. After worship time, ask them what happened or what they felt during worship time.

Small Group Activity: Bubbling

Supplies needed: bubbles for everyone

Have the students spend time playing with bubbles. Take this outside if possible. One way to save money and make great bubbles is to use a bowl of dishwashing liquid mixed with a little cornstarch. Then buy a wand for each student to dip into the solution.

Power Tools Part 3: Holy Spirit Power Lessons

Power Tools 3: Holy Spirit Power Lessons

The Holy Spirit Baptism

Acts 2:4 (NIV) *All of them were filled with the Holy Spirit and began to speak in other tongues as the Spirit enabled them.*

The Holy Spirit Makes Us Bold

Acts 1:8 (NIV) *But you shall receive power when the Holy Spirit has come upon you; and you shall be witnesses to Me in Jerusalem, and in all Judea and Samaria, and to the end of the earth.*

The Holy Spirit Helps Us

John 14:16 (NKJV) *And I will pray the Father, and He will give you another Helper, that He may abide with you forever.*

The Holy Spirit Reveals Things

Acts 2:17 (NIV) *"In the last days," God says, "I will pour out my Spirit on all people. Your sons and daughters will prophesy, your young men will see visions, your old men will dream dreams."*

The Holy Spirit Gives Us His Power

Zechariah 4:6b (NIV) *"Not by might nor by power, but by my Spirit," says the Lord Almighty.*

Lesson 1 - The Holy Spirit Baptism

Focus Point: Jesus wants to baptize us in the Holy Spirit

Goal: Students will learn who the Holy Spirit is, what the baptism of the Holy Spirit is, and will be encouraged to experience it for themselves.

Verse of the Day: Acts 2:4 (NIV) *All of them were filled with the Holy Spirit and began to speak in other tongues as the Spirit enabled them.*

Supplies Needed:

- doctor puppet or doctor costume for skit
- portable toolbox with various tools
- Tyler the Power Tool Guy Skit: Tyler wears a portable toolbox or toolbelt with various tools and is dressed in blue jeans and a plaid shirt, etc.
- drill or another power tool
- glass of water
- bowls of water
- small cups
- spoons
- 23 small round balloons
- magic markers
- packing tape
- pin or needle
- electric fan
- pictures of fire for each of your students and one for teacher (found in downloadable resources)
- adult headband
- clear drinking glass
- pitcher
- tiny doll or action figure that will fit in the drinking glass
- tray to catch excess water
- pitcher of water
- 5 paper or Styrofoam cups
- milk (optional)
- chocolate syrup (optional)
- spoon (optional)
- one piece of candy for each student

Opening: *Power Tools Countdown* or *Power Tools* Slide (Available free with registration of this curriculum.)

Welcome: The Holy Spirit

Supplies needed: glass of water

Welcome to Holy Spirit Power. For the next few weeks, we will learn about one of the most powerful tools in a Christian's life, the power of the Holy Spirit. God is one God but three parts. It's hard for even theologians to understand, but it's sort of like this glass of water. This is water also known as H2O. But if I were to heat this water to boiling, it would turn into steam. Yet, even though it's steam, it would still be H2O. If I were to freeze this water, it would turn into ice. But it would still be H2O. God the Father is God. God the Son is God. And God the Holy Spirit is God. They have different functions and personalities, but they are the same. They are one God just as this glass of water can become steam or ice is the same H2O.

You've probably already heard a lot about our Heavenly Father, God the Father. I'm sure you've heard a lot about God the Son, Jesus. For the next few weeks, we're going to learn more about God the Holy Spirit.

Prayer: Ask a child to pray over the service.

Rules: (use rules slide) Go over 5 Up rules.

Go over the *5 Ups Rules*: 1. Sit up straight. 2. Listen up. 3. Hush up. 4. Don't get up and run around or go to the bathroom. 5. Worship Up! (stand up and participate during praise and worship)

Theme or Activity Songs: Choose one of two fast moving activity or theme songs that go with the curriculum.

Game Time: Minute to Win It - Fill the cup (use game time slide)

Supplies Needed: bowls of water, small cups, spoons (You will need one set for each student participating in the game.)

This is a Minute to Win It Game, so you can use a minute countdown or a phone timer. Choose 2-4 students to participate. The goal of the game is to fill the cup with water. Using only a spoon, transfer the water from the bowl to the cup. If nobody manages to fill their cup by the time the minute is up, the student with the fullest cup wins.

I'm glad it's so much easier for the Holy Spirit to fill us than it is to fill these cups with water using only a spoon.

Memory Verse Skit: (use Holy Spirit Power Lesson 1, slide A)

Supplies needed: doctor puppet or doctor costume for skit

Doctor Word: Hi kids. I'm Doctor Word. I'm called that because I'm a doctor and because I love the Word of God. Many times, I have a patient who doesn't have insurance and can't afford the medicine prescribed to help his ailment. When that happens, I try to find medicine I can give him for free. Sometimes I'll have a sample the drug companies gave me, and I'll use those samples to give to these patients.

I'm glad none of us have to pay for the baptism of the Holy Spirit or work really hard to get it. The baptism of the Holy Spirit is a free gift to God's children when they seek Him. Our memory verse today talks about when the disciples in the Bible were first filled with the Holy Spirit.

Acts 2:4 (NIV) *All of them were filled with the Holy Spirit and began to speak in other tongues as the Spirit enabled them.*

Offering: Freely Give

Matthew 10:8 (NIV) says, "Freely you have received; freely give." What that means is because God has given us so much, including the baptism of the Holy Spirit, we shouldn't have a problem with freely giving in the offering.

Skit: Tyler the Power Tool Guy Renovates a House

Supplies Needed: Tyler has a portable toolbox or toolbelt with various tools and is dressed in blue jeans and a plaid shirt, etc., drill or another power tool. If you use a girl in the skit, have her dress the same and call her Tyler the Power Tool Gal.

(Tyler, the Power Tool Guy, comes into the room with a power tool. It doesn't matter which tool, but it should make noise when you start it up. A drill would work well.)

Leader: Hello, Power Tool Guy. So, how are you doing?

Tyler the Power Tool Guy: I'm doing great. I'm so excited. I can hardly wait.

Leader: I'm glad you're doing so great. What are you excited about?

Tyler: I just got the best job I've ever had.

Leader: That's wonderful. Does it pay better than the other jobs?

Tyler: Not really. The pay is about the same, but it has other perks.

Leader: That's great. I can see you're happy about it. What is this wonderful job?

Tyler: I get to renovate an old house.

Leader: Okay. What's so great about that job?

Tyler: Are you kidding? I get to tear down walls and cabinets and destroy things before I start putting in new stuff.

Leader: I'm happy for you. It sounds like fun.

Tyler: It is, but that's not all. I get to use almost all of my power tools on this job. (Starts power tool and revs it so it makes a lot of noise.) I feel so powerful.

Leader: That's awesome, Tyler. Today, we're talking about how to be powerful in our Christian lives.

Tyler: Do you get to tear things down and use power tools?

Leader: Not exactly. We get power through the baptism of the Holy Spirit.

Tyler: That's awesome. My power tools cost a lot of money. Do you have to pay anything or do anything to get Holy Spirit power.

Leader: Not a thing. The Holy Spirit comes to live inside of us when we get saved, and the baptism of the Holy Spirit is absolutely free for believers.

Tyler: Wow, that's amazing. I have to go make my plans for renovating the house now. Bye.

(Exits)

Verse of the Day: Acts 2:4 (NIV) *All of them were filled with the Holy Spirit and began to speak in other tongues as the Spirit enabled them.*

Memory Verse Talk: Filled with the Holy Spirit (use Holy Spirit Power Lesson 1, slide A)

Supplies needed: balloon

Speaking in tongues means speaking in a language we don't know. God gives us the words to speak when we are baptized in the Holy Spirit.

Have you ever wondered why people who are filled with the Holy Spirit speak in tongues? I used to wonder that until a minister told me that it's harder to control our words than any other part of the body. I believe that's true. When we become so yielded to the Holy Spirit that He controls what we say, even what language we say it in, that means we have allowed the Jesus to baptize in the Holy Spirit. We have given control of our tongues and our words to the Holy Spirit.

Blow up a balloon. *When I hold this blown-up balloon, I control it. I can move it anywhere I want. I can move it up, or I can move it down. But if I allow the balloon to have control, I don't know what this balloon is going to do.*

Let go of the balloon and let it fly off as the air escapes. *When I release my control, the Holy Spirit will do what He wants in my life just as the balloon does what it wants.*

The disciples in the Bible did just that. They let go of their control, and they allowed the Holy Spirit to control them. That's when they were filled and began to speak in other tongues.

Memory Verse Activity: Balloon Pop

Supplies needed: 22 balloons, magic markers, packing tape, pin or needle

Preparation: Blow up 22 balloons. Use the marker to write each word of the memory verse on a separate balloon. The address is also written on a balloon. Tape the balloons to the wall in order of the memory verse.

Warn the students ahead of time you are going to pop the balloons in case any of them are startled by the sound. Some may need to leave the room until you are done. Have students repeat the memory verse several times. As you pop each balloon, have the students say the memory verse again until there are no more balloons to pop.

Bible Story: The Upper Room

(Acts 2)

Supplies needed: powerful electric fan, headband with picture of fire taped onto it (picture found in downloadable resources)

Preparation: Choose 2-4 students to make fun and say, "You're drunk," at the appropriate time. Let the other students know to tell each other, "That's amazing," at the appropriate time.

Read the account in Acts 2 with the following instructions.

Acts 2:1 When the day of Pentecost came, they were all together in one place.

Acts 2:2 Suddenly a sound like the blowing of a violent wind came from heaven and filled the whole house where they were sitting. Turn on fan and blow it toward the students.

Acts 2:3 They saw what seemed to be tongues of fire that separated and came to rest on each of them. Place the fire headband with picture of fire on your head.

Acts 2:4 All of them were filled with the Holy Spirit and began to speak in other tongues as the Spirit enabled them. Explain to your students that speaking in tongues is speaking a language they don't know.

Acts 2:5-8, 11-12 Now there were staying in Jerusalem God-fearing Jews from every nation under heaven. When they heard this sound, a crowd came together in bewilderment, because each one heard their own language being spoken. Utterly amazed, they asked: "Aren't all these who are speaking Galileans? Then how is it that each of us hears them in our native language? ...we hear them declaring the wonders of God in our own tongues!" Amazed and perplexed, they asked one another, "What does this mean?" Have your students shrug their shoulders and say, "What could this mean to one another?"

Acts 2:13 Some, however, made fun of them and said, "They have had too much wine." Have the students you assigned to say, "You're drunk."

After this, Peter stood and addressed the crowd. He told them it was too early to be drunk, but this was prophesied in the Book of Joel. Then he spoke about how Jesus died and rose again to save them from their sins. The people asked Peter what they needed to do to be saved. Peter told them in verses 38-39.

Acts 2:38-39 Peter replied, "Repent and be baptized, every one of you, in the name of Jesus Christ for the forgiveness of your sins. And you will receive the gift of the Holy Spirit. The promise is for you and your children and for all who are far off—for all whom the Lord our God will call."

The baptism of the Holy Spirit was for them, but it's also for anyone who is a Christian – including children. Including each of you.

Praise and Worship: Choose a couple of fast song and a slow song to lead children into praise and worship. It works well to talk to the children about what worship is and why it's important before you enter into this time. You can have a children's praise team, but until they understand leading praise and worship, have an adult leader or yourself be the worship leader.

Video: Tongues or Shoes (available through downloadable resources)

Object Lessons:

5. 3 Baptisms

Supplies needed: clear glass, pitcher, tiny doll or action figure that will fit in a glass, tray to catch excess water

Sometimes we hear about baptism, and we think there is only one kind of baptism. That is when you go into the baptism pool and the pastor dunks you, but there are many types of baptism in your Christian life. I'm going to show you the three main baptisms available to every Christian.

When you are saved, the Holy Spirit comes to live inside you. Pour water into the glass. *When He does this, you become a Christian and are baptized into the body of Christ.*

Then there is baptism in water. After you become a Christian, at some point, you are baptized in water. That shows to everyone that you made a commitment to give your life to Christ. It doesn't make you a Christian, but it shows you are a Christian. Hold the doll above the water. *When you are baptized, you are showing that Christ died for your sins,* Dunk the doll in the glass of water above its head. *Christ was buried.* Raise the doll back out of the water. *Then Christ rose again defeating sin and death.*

Have a helper or a child demonstrate what would happen to someone baptized in water at your church. Emphasize that the child would be warned and have time to hold his breath, and the pastor wouldn't keep him under the water for more than a couple of seconds. Have your students hold their breaths for ten seconds to show how they can all hold their breaths longer than they would need to during the baptism. Answer any questions they might have about water baptism. Encourage your students to get baptized at the next opportunity the church gives. You may want to discuss this with your pastor so he can schedule a baptism.

As you say this next part, continue to pour water in the cup until it overflows. *There are many other baptisms. There's a baptism of fire, a baptism of peace, a baptism of joy, and others. God fills us often if we allow Him too. Then there is the baptism of the Holy Spirit. This happens when you are completely yielded to the Holy Spirit.* Hold up the glass of water. *It's like taking this glass of water and throwing it into the middle of the ocean. You won't know where the water in the glass starts or ends. It will be a part of the ocean. That's the baptism of the Holy Spirit. The first evidence that you've received the baptism of the Holy Spirit is when you begin to speak in other languages or tongue. Sometimes it will be gibberish at first, just as a baby talks gibberish when he's learning to talk, but as you continue to be filled, your prayer language will grow.*

6.   Who Can Receive the Baptism of the Holy Spirit?

Supplies needed: pitcher of water, 5 paper or Styrofoam cups, tray or bowl to catch excess water

Preparation: First cup is turned upside down. Second cup has dirt, trash, and mud in it. Third cup has holes in the bottom. Fourth cup is cut in half length wise with the cup side turned toward the children. Fifth cup is right side up and has nothing in it.

Even though the Baptism of the Holy Spirit is a free gift that God wants to give His children, there

are ways to prepare to receive this free gift.

Pour water on the first cup. *This represents a child who has not asked Jesus Christ into His heart. Since he doesn't know Christ as his Savior, he can't receive the baptism of the Holy Spirit.*

Show your students the inside of the second cup. *This child can't receive the baptism of the Holy Spirit because he has sin in his life. He needs to confess his sin to God and ask God to forgive him before he receives the baptism of the Holy Spirit.*

Pour water in the third cup. *This child is saved and has been forgiven of his sin, but he can't receive the baptism of the Holy Spirit because he doesn't have faith that God will fill Him. Maybe he thinks he's too young or not good enough. Or maybe he believes that God only wants to fill people like the preacher and the children's pastor. He needs to plug the holes in his faith. The way to do that is learn about the Holy Spirit from the Bible, then seek the Holy Spirit. Before long, those faith holes will be plugged up.*

Pour water in the fourth cup. *This child can't receive the Holy Spirit because he hasn't surrendered himself completely to God. We all spend a lifetime giving ourselves to God. It will never be complete, but to receive the baptism of the Holy Spirit, we need to be open to God and commit our lives to Him. We need to be thirsty for more of Him.*

Pour water into the fifth cup until it overflows. *God wants to fill you with the baptism of the Holy Spirit.*

Lead the students in a prayer that addresses each of the children represented by the different cups.

Optional Object Lesson: Stir Up the Holy Spirit

Supplies needed: glass, milk, chocolate syrup, spoon

Pour milk in the glass. *The milk represents us. When we get saved, the Holy Spirit comes to live inside of us.* Pour chocolate syrup in milk. *Even though this milk has the chocolate in it, the chocolate has not taken over every part of the milk. When we are saved, the Holy Spirit comes to live inside of us. He guides us, comforts us, and shows us when we sin and need to ask God's forgiveness, but we aren't fully taken over by the Holy Spirit. We need to stir up the gift of the Holy Spirit within us.*

Stir the chocolate milk. *As I stir this milk, the chocolate seeps into every part of it. You can't say this part is chocolate and this part is milk because it is all chocolate milk. That's the way it is when we stir up the Holy Spirit inside of us, and He baptizes us in the Holy Spirit.*

Now, what happens if we set the chocolate milk in the refrigerator and leave it for a few days. Allow the students to answer. *The milk and the chocolate separate. You begin to see what part is milk and what part is chocolate. That's why it is important to continue to stir up the gift and keep being filled with the Holy Spirit.* Take a drink of the milk. *Hmm. Taste and see that the Lord is good.*

Message: How to Receive the Free Gift

Supplies needed: one piece of candy for each student

Give each student a piece of candy. Unless your church's guidelines don't permit it, allow your students to eat the candy while you're talking.

Have someone in your church give a testimony about being baptized in the Holy Spirit as a child. If you have children in your ministry who were baptized in the Holy Spirit, have them talk about their experience. If you were baptized in the Holy Spirit as a child, you may also want to give your testimony.

Ask the students what they had to do to receive the candy they're eating. They may answer that they didn't have to do anything, or they had to reach out and grab it. Tell the children that the baptism of the Holy Spirit is a free gift they only need to reach out and grab it.

In a moment, we're going to take some time to worship God and allow His Holy Spirit to move. Some of you may not be ready to receive the baptism of the Holy Spirit yet, and that's okay. You can take your time and learn more before you decide, but you can still spend time worshipping and seeking God today. The Holy Spirit may decide to baptize you with His joy or His peace today. We're going to believe that God will baptize those who want it with the Holy Spirit. Here's how you can grab hold of the baptism of the Holy Spirit just as you grabbed hold of the free candy.

1. Ask Jesus for the baptism of the Holy Spirit. Once you've asked Jesus to baptize you in the Holy Spirit, He will do it. Even if it doesn't happen right away, God will fulfill His promises. Let's take a moment to pray and ask Jesus to baptize us in the Holy Spirit.

2. Praise God out loud using your voices. God doesn't zap you against your will to get you to speak in tongues. God uses your voices, but it is Him speaking through you. Use your voices to praise God out loud, and let Him do the rest. That doesn't mean you have to shout, but you can. As long as you speak loud enough for you to hear yourself, He can fill you. You might want to say things like, "Hallelujah. I love you, Jesus. I want more of you, Holy Spirit. Praise you, Lord."

3. Surrender your words. When you start to feel your tongues and mouths forming in strange ways, surrender your words to God and allow Him to speak through you.

4. Wait on God. Sometimes you aren't baptized in the Holy Spirit right away. God wants to fill you. Keep seeking Him and praising him, and it will happen. Sometimes, it's hard to concentrate on God when all these people are around, but you don't have to be in church to be baptized in the Holy Spirit. It might happen today while you're at home or tonight while you're in your bed praising God.

Response Time:

Encourage the children to come to the front to worship God. You may want to ask the children seeking the baptism of the Holy Spirit to stand in one area. Play worship music and encourage all the children to worship God using their voices. When you see God moving on certain children, lay your hand gently on their heads. Don't pray loudly over them because you might distract them. Allow the Holy Spirit to do the work. Instruct them only if you feel led by the Holy Spirit to do so.

After the response time, ask the students if any of them were baptized in the Holy Spirit. Encourage them to continue to seek the Holy Spirit and learn more about Him.

Small Group Activity: Fire Headband Craft

Supplies needed: child's headband or yarn for each student, fire picture for each student (found in downloadable resources), tape, scissors

Have each student cut out the fire picture, then tape it to their headbands or yarn they will tie around their heads. Now they have a reminder to wear about being baptized in the Holy Spirit. While the students are doing the craft, ask them if they have any questions about the baptism of the Holy Spirit. Tell them about your experiences with the Holy Spirit.

Lesson 2 - The Holy Spirit Makes Us Bold

Focus Point: The Holy Spirit makes us bold.

Goal: The students will learn being filled with the Holy Spirit will give them the boldness they need to share the Gospel.

Verse of the Day: Acts 1:8 (NIV) *But you shall receive power when the Holy Spirit has come upon you; and you shall be witnesses to Me in Jerusalem, and in all Judea and Samaria, and to the end of the earth.*

Supplies Needed:

- doctor puppet or doctor costume for skit
- portable toolbox with various tools
- Tyler the Power Tool Guy Skit: Tyler wears a portable toolbox or toolbelt with various tools and is dressed in blue jeans and a plaid shirt, etc.
- sledge hammer or chain saw
- plastic eggs
- strips of paper
- rubber chicken
- rubber boat or toy that floats
- clear small bowl filled halfway with water
- pitcher of water
- tray to catch excess water
- flashlight
- batteries
- Steve Spangler Science Energy Stick (optional)

Opening: *Power Tools Countdown* (optional) or *Power Tools* Slide

Welcome: Be Bold

Welcome children. Today, we're going to learn about being bold in the power of the Holy Spirit. One definition of bold is to be fearless in the face of danger. Many of the early church leaders had that kind of boldness. Missionaries who go to foreign lands also have that kind of boldness. All of us need that boldness in our every day lives. We need that boldness in our homes, our schools, and in our neighborhoods so we can share the Gospel of Christ and live a Christian life that pleases God. Even if you are naturally shy, the Holy Spirit will give you the boldness you need.

Prayer: Ask a child to pray over the service.

Rules: (use rules slide) Go over the 5 Ups Rules.

Go over the *5 Ups Rules*: 1. Sit up straight. 2. Listen up. 3. Hush up. 4. Don't get up and run around or

91

go to the bathroom. 5. Worship Up! (stand up and participate during praise and worship)

Theme or Activity Songs: Choose one of two fast moving activity or theme songs that go with the curriculum.

Game Time: Chicken, Chicken, Rooster (use game time slide)

Supplies needed: none

Play this game like Duck, Duck, Goose, but have the students say, *Chicken, Chicken, Rooster* instead. This is normally a pre-school game, but have fun with it.

Have the students sit in a circle. The student who is it goes around the circle and taps each child saying, "Chicken." When a student is tapped and the person who is it says, "Rooster," the tapped student must run after the student who is it and tap that person before he sits in the place of the student who was tapped. If the tapped student fails, he's it. Play several times.

The student who was tapped had to show boldness chasing the student who was it. The Holy Spirit wants to take the chicken out of us and give us boldness when we tell others about Jesus.

Memory Verse Skit: (use Holy Spirit Power Lesson 2, slide A)

Supplies needed: doctor puppet or doctor costume for skit

Doctor Word: Hi kids. I'm Doctor Word. I'm called that because I'm a doctor and because I love the Word of God. When I first became a doctor, I was always worried I might make a mistake. In most professions, people make mistakes, and it doesn't matter that much. But when a doctor makes a mistake, it can have life-threatening consequences. Because I was so afraid of making a mistake, sometimes I didn't diagnose illnesses right away. This caused problems for my patients. I didn't know how to fix my problem, so I prayed about it. Jesus filled me with the Holy Spirit, and things changed. The Holy Spirit gave me boldness to treat patients in the right way. I became a better doctor. Because of this, I was able to go on mission's trips to other countries. I would treat their illnesses and share the Gospel of Jesus Christ with them. That's why today's memory verse is so important. Acts 1:8 (NIV) says, *"But you shall receive power when the Holy Spirit has come upon you; and you shall be witnesses to Me in Jerusalem, and in all Judea and Samaria, and to the end of the earth."* One type of power the Holy Spirit gives us is boldness. I'm so glad He gave me the boldness I needed.

Offering: Giving Boldly

2 Corinthians 3:12 (NIV) says, "Therefore, since we have such a hope, we are very bold." In other words, because Christ gives us hope, and because we have the Holy Spirit inside of us, we can do everything with boldness. We can even give in the offering with boldness. Let's give boldly today.

If you have a mission's project your church supports, this would be a great time to tell your students about the bold missionaries and take a mission's offering.

Have a child pray over the offering.

Skit: Tyler the Power Tool Guy Boldly Demolishes

Supplies needed: sledge hammer or chain saw. Tyler has a portable toolbox or toolbelt with various tools and is dressed in blue jeans and a plaid shirt, etc. If you use a girl in the skit, have her dress the same and call her Tyler the Power Tool Gal.

Tyler the Power Tool Guy: (Comes in whistling or humming)

Leader: You sound happy, Tyler. Did you start on your job remodeling that house?

Tyler: I sure did, and I'm using tools like this to demolish walls and cabinets I no longer need.

Leader: So, you like to demolish houses.

Tyler: I didn't at first, but now I love it.

Leader: Why didn't you like it at first?

Tyler: It took me forever to tear down a wall or rip out a cabinet, but now I know the secret to get it done faster.

Leader: Really? What secret is that?

Tyler: I was using this tool too timidly like I might break something. I learned I have to demolish with boldness and power, or I won't be effective.

Leader: That's interesting. Today, we're learning how the Holy Spirit gives us boldness to tell others about Jesus.

Tyler: I never thought that the Holy Spirit and house renovation were so much alike. I have some work to do. See you next week. Bye.

Verse of the Day: Acts 1:8 (NIV) *But you shall receive power when the Holy Spirit has come upon you; and you shall be witnesses to Me in Jerusalem, and in all Judea and Samaria, and to the end of the earth.*

Memory Verse Talk: (use Holy Spirit Power Lesson 2, slide A)

One purpose of the baptism of the Holy Spirit is to give us power or boldness when we witness to others about our faith in Jesus Christ. Sometimes telling others about Jesus can make us timid or afraid, but the Holy Spirit can help us by giving us the words to say and the opportunities to say them. This verse also tells us where we should be witnesses for Christ. Most of us have never been to these places, but Jesus was speaking to the disciples who lived in Jerusalem. So we can insert places we know. For instance, Jerusalem would be places we are at all the time like our homes, our schools, and our neighborhoods. Judea would be like our city. So, we might find opportunities to witness to people in our city who don't go to our schools or live in our neighborhoods. Samaria would be the outsiders. Maybe there's a student at school that everyone picks on or someone with a disability, and nobody sits with him at lunch. These are also people we should find opportunities to tell about Jesus' love. The uttermost parts of the Earth means everywhere else. Some of you might grow up and take missions trips to other countries or become full-time missionaries. Even if you don't, you can pray for missionaries and give offerings for missions.

Memory Verse Activity: Chicken Egg Roll (use Holy Spirit Power Lesson 2, slide A)

Supplies needed: plastic eggs, strips of paper

Preparation: Place a slip of paper in each egg with words or phrases from the memory verse. Split the verses up depending on the number of students participating. If you have a larger group, you can split the students into different teams.

Each student will be given an egg. When the race begins, the student will roll the egg to the finish line with his or her nose (beak) only. When all the students finish, they will place the pieces of paper in order to show the memory verse.

Bible Story: The Holy Spirit Takes the Chicken Out of Peter

(Luke 22:31-34, 54-62; Acts 2:1-41)

Supplies needed: rubber chicken

When Jesus lived on the Earth, Peter was one of His most loyal disciples. Peter would do anything for Jesus. Shortly before Jesus was arrested, He told Peter that Peter would deny Him three times before the rooster crowed twice.

Peter was shocked. He told Jesus that even if everyone else deserted Him, Peter would go with Him even if it cost his life. Peter meant what he said. He loved Jesus and wanted to support Him, even if it cost Peter his life, but something happened.

Jesus was arrested and taken to trial. Peter followed and stood in the courtyard trying to figure out a way to help Jesus, but Peter was scared. Have you ever been so scared that you couldn't do something you really wanted to do? I believe we all have been that scared. Peter was afraid he was going to be arrested and killed. He stood around the fire hoping nobody recognized him.

That's when a young servant girl saw him. "This one has been with Jesus."

Peter was so terrified, he lied and said he didn't even know Jesus.

Another person came up to Peter and accused him of being one of Jesus' followers. Peter denied it again.

An hour passed, and Peter probably was starting to relax again when another person came up to him and accused him of being with Jesus. At this point, Peter was so afraid he swore and said he'd never heard of Jesus.

At that point, three things happened. First the rooster crowed twice. Then, as Jesus was marched through the courtyard by the soldiers, He looked at Peter. Peter was so distraught, he ran away and cried bitterly. When it had really mattered, he was a chicken and didn't stand with Jesus. Squeeze the rubber chicken.

After Jesus rose from the grave, He forgave Peter. A few weeks later, Peter was in the upper room where he and the other disciples were baptized in the Holy Spirit. When that happened, the Holy Spirit took the chicken out of Peter. Squeeze the rubber chicken.

He stood and witnessed to the whole crowd. Not only did he do that, but he told them that they were guilty of crucifying the Son of God. The people asked him what they could do, and Peter told them in Acts 2:28 (NKJV), "Repent, and let every one of you be baptized in the name of Jesus Christ for the remission of sins; and you shall receive the gift of the Holy Spirit."

Peter lived the rest of his life fearlessly telling other people about Jesus. When you're baptized in the Holy Spirit, the Holy Spirit will take the chicken out of you like he did for Peter and help you become a bold witness for Him.

Praise and Worship: Choose a couple of fast song and a slow song to lead children into praise and worship. It works well to talk to the children about what worship is and why it's important before you enter into this time. You can have a children's praise team, but until they understand leading praise and worship, have an adult leader or yourself be the worship leader.

Object Lesson:

5. The Holy Spirit is Stronger Than Our Fears

Supplies needed: rubber boat or toy that float, clear small bowl filled halfway with water, pitcher of water, tray to catch excess water

Have you ever been afraid of anything? What were you afraid of? Allow students to answer. *Those are some scary things.* Tell the students about things you were afraid of when you were younger.

Fear can be a good thing. We don't jump over a cliff because we're afraid of falling. We don't pick up poisonous snakes because we're afraid of getting bit. We don't touch hot stoves or fire because we're afraid of getting burned. Those are healthy fears that keep us safe. Fear is only bad when it's an unhealthy fear, when we're afraid of something that isn't really harmful, or when we don't do what God wants us to do because we're afraid. Those are the kind of fears the Holy Spirit can help us with.

Can you think of fears like that? Allow students to answer. If they can't think of any, make some suggestions.

Show the students the toy boat. *I'm going to call this boat the fear boat. Pretend this boat is full of all of your unhealthy fears.* Place the boat in the bowl of water. Start pouring the pitcher of water into the bowl. As you do this, continue talking. *The more we are filled with the Holy Spirit, the more the Holy Spirit will wash those fears away.* Keep pouring the water until the boat floats outside of the bowl.

6. The Power to Be Bold

Supplies needed: flashlight, batteries

Preparation: Make sure the batteries are not in the flashlight.

Have you ever been afraid of the dark? When I was young and my mom turned out the lights, I used to worry that a monster would come out of the shadows and get me. My mom gave me a flashlight so I could turn it on when I was afraid. Whenever I turned on the flashlight, I saw there weren't really monsters in my room.

Without Jesus in their lives, the people around me live in a dark world. There are times I really want to be a bold witness for Christ. I want my light to shine in the darkness, so I have here my trusty flashlight. Show flashlight. *I can shine this flashlight in the darkest of places, and it will light things up. When things are dark, I'm more likely to be afraid, but when things are lit up, my fears go away. That's because the light of the Holy Spirit overcomes the darkness.*

Turn on flashlight. *I don't understand. Nothing happened. This flashlight should have the power to shine boldly in the darkness, but it doesn't. Do any of you have an idea what might be wrong?* Allow students to answer until one of the students says to check the batteries. Open up the flashlight and show there aren't any batteries in it.

No wonder my flashlight won't work. I don't have batteries in it. It's the batteries that give a flashlight the power to shine. Place the batteries in the flashlight and turn it on.

Just as the flashlight needs batteries to power it, I need the Holy Spirit to give me the power to be a light for Jesus in this dark world. Without the power of the Holy Spirit, I can't be a bold witness. I can't let my light shine.

Optional Object Lesson: Stay Connected to the Holy Spirit

Supplies needed: Steve Spangler Science Energy Stick

Have the students make an open circle. Place the energy stick in one hand and hold onto the hand of one of the students. Make sure the circle is open, and two people in the circle aren't holding hands. Have the students not holding hands close the circle by holding hands. The energy stick should light up.

When we are baptized in the Holy Spirit and are connected to Him, He gives us the power to become bold witnesses. But it's important to keep that connection and continually allow the Holy Spirit to fill you. If you break the connection, the Holy Spirit will no longer give you the boldness you need. Have two of the students in the circle break the circle by letting go of each other's hands.

We need to stay connected to the Holy Spirit. Have them hold hands again and complete the circle.

Message: The Holy Spirit Will Take the Chicken Out of You

(use Holy Spirit Power Lesson 2, slide B)

Supplies needed: rubber chicken

It's great to say that the Holy Spirit will take the chicken out of you, but it's harder when you want to talk to someone about Jesus and are afraid. What do you do when you're afraid that person might make fun of you? What about if it's in school and the teacher tells you that you can't talk about Jesus? What if your friend won't be your friend if you keep talking about Jesus? These are real things that can make you scared of telling others about Jesus. Those things have a spirit of fear on them. Squeeze rubber chicken.

Even though the spirit of fear can be strong, the Holy Spirit overcomes our fear and gives us boldness.

Show slide B and read the following verse. *2 Timothy 1:7 (NKJV) For God has not given us a spirit of fear, but of power and of love and of a sound mind.*

The Holy Spirit can give us the power to speak even when we are afraid. He conquers the spirit of fear because He is more powerful. He'll get rid of our fear. Another way to say it is the Holy Spirit will take the chicken in us. Throw the chicken over your shoulder.

The Holy Spirit is always with you. He is more powerful than any fear. Let me give you an example.

For this example, choose a young student and an older student. Ask a large adult from your church to help you with this example.

Have the young student stand out front. *Let's pretend this student wants to witness to her friends, but she's afraid. There's a bully in school who doesn't like Christians and gets other kids to make fun of them.*

Have the older student act threatening. *The younger student is afraid, she knows that the Holy Spirit lives inside of her. First, she prays.* Instruct the student to tell God she's afraid and that she needs the Holy Spirit to help you.

If she's baptized in the Holy Spirit, she'll begin to speak in tongues and worship to strengthen her inner spirit. She'll also remind herself that the Holy Spirit is more powerful than her fear. She'll say Bible verses like 1 John 4:4, "Greater is He that is within me than He that is in the world." Have the younger student repeat that phrase three or four times with convictions.

At this point, the large adult will stand in front of the smaller student and block the other student from getting to her. Encourage the other student not to give up, but the adult will always block him.

The Holy Spirit is greater than any fear or any bully that could come against us. Let's repeat 1 John 4:4 and shout like we really mean it. Have the students repeat "Greater is He that is within me than He that is within the world five or six times. Encourage them to shout the words.

Response Time

For response time, encourage students to be filled or refilled with the Holy Spirit. Play worship music, and lay hands on the students as you see God moving upon them. After worship, recap what God did for them.

Small Group Chat: Fear Not Picture Frames

Supplies needed: copies of Fear Not verses from Holy Spirit Power downloadable resources, cardstock, craft foam or optional craft picture frames, glue, markers, sticker, various craft decorations

Preparations: Make a copy of Fear Not verses for each student. Use 8 ½ by 11 inch size cardstock to glue Fear Not verses papers. Make sure they are centered on the cardstock.

Have students cut out and glue craft foam around the edges of the card stock to create a picture frame. Let them decorate their frames.

While the students are decorating their picture frames, go over the Fear Not verses. Let the students know they can hang these verses in their bedrooms or in their lockers at school to remind them the

Holy Spirit is with them, and they don't have to be afraid.

Lesson 3 - The Holy Spirit Helps Us

Focus Point: The Holy Spirit helps us.

Goal: Students will learn that the Holy Spirit was sent by God to come alongside us and help us in a variety of ways.

Verse of the Day: John 14:16 (NKJV) *And I will pray the Father, and He will give you another Helper, that He may abide with you forever.*

Supplies Needed:

- doctor puppet or doctor costume for skit
- portable toolbox with various tools
- Tyler the Power Tool Guy Skit: Tyler wears a portable toolbox or toolbelt with various tools and is dressed in blue jeans and a plaid shirt, etc.
- blueprints
- chairs
- Signs with the following written on them with a colorful marker: Holy Spirit Boldness, Holy Spirit Knowledge, Holy Spirit Wisdom, Holy Spirit Deliverance
- drinking straw
- string
- tape
- balloon
- ink pad
- paper
- wipe
- tennis racket or other sports equipment

Opening: *Power Tools Countdown* (optional) or *Power Tools* Slide

Welcome:

Welcome. This month, we've been learning about the Holy Spirit. Today, we're going to learn about one of the main jobs of the Holy Spirit. The Holy Spirit lives in us to help us. There are many ways the Holy Spirit helps us, and we're going to learn some of those ways in this lesson.

Prayer: Ask a child to pray over the service.

Rules: (use rules slide) Go over the 5 Ups Rules.

Go over the *5 Ups Rules*: 1. Sit up straight. 2. Listen up. 3. Hush up. 4. Don't get up and run around or go to the bathroom. 5. Worship Up! (stand up and participate during praise and worship)

Theme or Activity Songs: Choose one of two fast moving activity or theme songs that go with the curriculum.

Game Time: Fruit Basket (use game time slide)

Supplies needed: chairs

Preparation: Arrange chairs in a circle facing the center. Have one chair for each student.

Stand in the center of the circle and have the students sit in the chairs. Assign each player to be a fruit. Have three or more fruits to assign. It is preferable to have at least three to five students be assigned to each fruit. Increase the number of fruits to accomplish that. Encourage the students to remember which fruit they are.

The object of the game is to have the center person call out the name of a fruit. All students who were assigned that fruit must stand and find another seat. You call out the fruit first and sit so one of the students doesn't have a chair to sit in. That student is the next to call out a fruit.

When the students get the hang of the game, stand and allow all the students to sit. Explain that when Fruit Basket is called out, all of the students must find another seat. Let them know they can't sit in the seat next to them. Call out Fruit Basket, and sit in one of the seats. Continue the game.

One way the Holy Spirit helps us is to enable us to make us fruity Christian. The Holy Spirt fruit that He wants us to have is love, joy, peace, longsuffering, goodness, kindness, faithfulness, gentleness, and self-control. The more we allow the Holy Spirit to fill us and help us, the more this fruit will show in our lives.

Memory Verse Skit: (use Holy Spirit Power Lesson 3, slide A)

Supplies needed: doctor puppet or doctor costume for skit

Doctor Word: Hi kids. I'm Doctor Word. I'm called that because I'm a doctor and because I love the Word of God. Being a doctor is a difficult job. I have to remember a lot of things I learned in medical school. I have to remember the symptoms for every disease and how to treat the disease once I diagnose it. I'm so grateful I have the Holy Spirit to help and guide me along the way. When I'm treating a patient, I sometimes feel the Holy Spirit has come alongside me to help me know what to do. That's why today's memory verse is so important to me. John 14:16 (NKJV) says, *"And I will pray the Father, and He will give you another Helper, that He may abide with you forever."* Imagine that. Jesus prayed for us to have the Holy Spirit to stay with us forever and to help us. That's comforting.

Offering: The Holy Spirit Helps Us Know What to Give

Did you know the Holy Spirit can help you know how much to give? Tell a story about how the Holy Spirit urged you to give a certain amount in the offering, and how it impacted you. Or tell how you needed something (food, money), and the Holy Spirit urged someone else to give you just what you needed.

Skit: Tyler the Power Tool Guy Has a Plan

Supplies Needed: blueprints or plans. Tyler has a portable toolbox or toolbelt with various tools and is dressed in blue jeans and a plaid shirt, etc. If you use a girl in the skit, have her dress the same and call her Tyler the Power Tool Gal.

Tyler the Power Tool Guy: (Comes in and starts pouring over plans) Okay, if I extended it here, I'd have to decrease it there.

Leader: Hi, Tyler. What's going on? Do you have any special power tools to show us today?

Tyler: Not today. Today, I have something much more powerful than a power tool.

Leader: More powerful than a power tool? I can't believe you said that. What is this thing more powerful than a power tool?

Tyler: I have the blueprints to the house I'm renovating and the plans for what I'm going my renovation.

Leader: How are those papers more important than a power tool?

Tyler: These plans and blueprints guide and help me. If I build an island and don't look at the plans first, the island might be too big to fit in the kitchen. Or I might buy a bathtub that's two inches too long for the bathtub area.

Leader: I never thought of that.

Tyler: These plans help me in other ways too. Suppose I want to tear down a wall. If the wall is load bearing, meaning it supports the whole upstairs, I can't tear it down without installing a beam to support it. Having these plans to help and guide me is the most important part of renovating a house.

Leader: So, those plans are sort of like the Holy Spirit.

Tyler: How can house plans be like the Holy Spirit.

Leader: The Holy Spirit guides us and helps us in every area of our life. He even helps us understand the Bible.

Tyler: In that case, you're right. The Holy Spirit is like these house plans. I have to go. I'm meeting with the project manager to go over these plans.

(Exits)

Verse of the Day: John 14:16 (NKJV) *And I will pray the Father, and He will give you another Helper, that He may abide with you forever.*

Memory Verse Talk: (use Holy Spirit Power Lesson 3, slide A)

Imagine having someone come alongside you all the time and help you whenever you need it. When you need to remember something, that helper will help you remember. When you need strength or the ability to do something, that helper will give you that ability. When you are upset, that helper will comfort you. When you need wisdom or guidance, that helper will guide you. When you need to know the right thing to do, the helper will let you know.

It doesn't take much to imagine this because if you're a Christian, you already have a helper like this. The Holy Spirit is your helper who is always with you.

Memory Verse Activity: Help Each Other

Have your students pair up. Each pair should have an older student and a younger student. The older student teaches the younger student the verse. When you're done, have the younger students say the verse.

I split you into pairs so one of you could help the other learn the memory verse. Was this helpful? Allow students to answer. *The Holy Spirit also wants to help you remember Scripture because The Holy Spirit is always with us to help us.*

Bible Story: The Holy Spirit Helps Peter and John

(Acts 4:1-31)

Supplies needed: Signs with the following written on them with a colorful marker: Holy Spirit Boldness, Holy Spirit Knowledge, Holy Spirit Wisdom, Holy Spirit Deliverance. Write in pencil on the back what each sign says so you can easily find the right sign.

The disciples, Peter and John, went to the temple and found a crippled man there. They healed him in the name of Jesus, and he started walking, leaping and praising God. This made everyone interested in hearing what Peter and John had to say, so they preached the Gospel.

Soon, they were arrested and brought before the temple leaders. They weren't arrested for stealing or hurting others. They were arrested because they were doing something good. They were telling others about Jesus and how He died for our sins and rose again. Some people listened to Peter and John and invited Jesus to be their Savior and Lord. This made the temple leaders angry. That's why they arrested Peter and John. They put them in prison overnight.

Ask the students if they've ever been told they can't talk about Jesus. The students who go to public school have probably been told this at some point.

The next day, the leaders brought in Peter and John and questioned them. They asked, "By what power or what name did you do this?"

Show Holy Spirit Boldness sign.

Scripture says that Peter was filled with the Holy Spirit and stood up to the leaders even though they might send him to prison. He told them all about Jesus and how they had healed a lame man in the name of Jesus.

Show Holy Spirit Knowledge sign.

The leaders were amazed. They knew Peter and John weren't educated men, but they knew the Scriptures and what they meant. This was because the Holy Spirit helped them by teaching them about God's Word.

Show Holy Spirit Wisdom sign.

The leaders threatened Peter and John and told them not to teach or preach in the name of Jesus again. The Holy Spirit helped Peter and John by giving them wisdom about what to say. In Acts 4:19-20 (NIV), But Peter and John replied, "Which is right in God's eyes: to listen to you, or to him? You be the judges! As for us, we cannot help speaking about what we have seen and heard."

Show Holy Spirit Deliverance sign.

The Holy Spirit helped Peter and John by delivered them from prison. The temple leaders couldn't figure out how to punish them since a man had been miraculously healed, so they let them go.

In difficult times, the Holy Spirit will help you just as He helped Peter and John.

Praise and Worship: Choose a couple of fast song and a slow song to lead children into praise and worship. It works well to talk to the children about what worship is and why it's important before you enter into this time. You can have a children's praise team, but until they understand leading praise and worship, have an adult leader or yourself be the worship leader.

Object Lessons:

5. The Holy Spirit Guides Us (use Holy Spirit Lesson 3, slides B, C, D, and E)

Supplies needed: drinking straw, string, tape, balloon, ink pad, paper, wipe

Preparation: Thread the string through the straw before the demonstration.

Show Slide B. *One way the Holy Spirit helps us is by guiding us into all truth. John 16:13 (NIV) says, "But when he, the Spirit of truth, comes, he will guide you into all the truth."*

Give an illustration about how that happens. Choose two students to help you. One student will hold one end of the string. Blow up the balloon or have the other student blow it up. Tell the student to aim it at the other student and let go. The balloon will not reach its target. Have the student try a couple more times. Explain that, without the Holy Spirit guiding us, we can't get where we need to be.

Blow the balloon up again. This time, tape it to the straw. Explain that the straw acts in the same way as the Holy Spirit. Hold on to the other end of the string, and have the student let go of the balloon. The balloon will reach the other student. *The Holy Spirit will guide you if you let Him.*

Sometimes, Christians have a hard time understanding how the Holy Spirit can guide us when He doesn't speak out loud and we can't see Him. We tell you to listen to the Holy Spirit and do what He tells you, but sometimes, we forget to tell you how to listen to the Holy Spirit. The Holy Spirit rarely speaks in a voice you can hear out loud, but He lives inside your spirit, and He does speak to our spirit and impress things upon us.

Show the students the stamp pad. Place your finger on the pad and press it onto the paper. Show the students your fingerprint. Use the wipe to wipe the ink off your finger. *I have an impression of my finger on this paper. It doesn't look exactly like my finger, but it does show the imprint of my finger. It's my fingerprint. An impression is sort of like that. The Holy Spirit impresses something on the inside of you. You don't have a clear picture of what He wants, but you do have an impression. From that impression, you can figure out how the Holy Spirit wants to guide you. You have a Holy Spirit print on your spirit.*

Show slide C. *One way the Holy Spirit guides us or impresses us is to help us understand God's Word. John 14:26 (NIV) say, "But the Advocate, the Holy Spirit, whom the Father will send in my name, will teach you all things and will remind you of everything I have said to you." Sometimes, He'll remind us what the Word of God says. Other times, He'll show us what the verses mean.*

Another way the Holy Spirit guides us is to bears witness with our spirits so we know what is right and what is wrong. Some people say you should let your conscious be your guide. That works most of the time when we know what is right and what is wrong, but sometimes we need help.

Show Slide D. Ezekiel 36:27 (NIV) says, "I will put my Spirit inside you. And I will help you live by my rules. You will be careful to obey my laws."

The Holy Spirit does that in two ways. First, He'll show you what is right and what is wrong. Second, He'll show you when you've done something wrong so you can ask God to forgive you.

A third way the Holy Spirit guides us is to give us wisdom. Wisdom is different than knowledge. Knowledge is knowing facts. Wisdom shows us what to do in hard situations.

Show Slide E. *James 1:5 (NIV) says, "If any of you lacks wisdom, you should ask God, who gives generously to all without finding fault, and it will be given to you."*

So if you don't know what to do, you can ask the Holy Spirit, and He will guide you with His wisdom.

6. Object Lesson: The Holy Spirit Comforts Us

Supplies needed: comforter or blanket

Have your students raise their hands if any of the following things have happened to them.

Have you ever been sad? Have you ever had a pet or a grandparent or someone close to you die? Have you even been upset because you lost a friend either because the friend moved away or because he stopped being your friend? Have you ever heard your parents yell at each other, and it scared you? Have you ever had a bad dream? Have you ever had anyone bully you? Have you ever been sick? Have you ever been accused of doing something you didn't do? Have you ever been treated unfairly?

Here's the last question. Raise your hand if you would answer yes to any of these questions? Keep your hands raised and look around. All of us have had many of these things happen to us.

This is my comforter from when I was little. Tell a story about when you were little how getting under a blanket of comforter would make you feel better when you were upset, or sick, or sad, or even angry. *Some children use blankets or comforters to make a tent over a table or a desk. They feel safe and comforted hiding under their tent blankets. Some don't use comforters. They hug stuffed animals, or they go to a special place in their yard or home that makes them feel better. Some like to listen to music, read stories, and draw pictures.*

How many of you have something you use to comfort you? Allow student to answer. Ask the students who want to what they use to comfort them.

All those things you mentioned are wonderful comforters, but the Holy Spirit is even a better comforter. Tell about a time in your life when the Holy Spirit comforted you during a hard time. *The Holy Spirit makes you feel better when you're sad, and He heals those sad feelings. He can even help you know how to handle these bad situations. The Holy Spirit is the best comforter there is.*

Message: The Holy Spirit Helps Us

Supplies needed: tennis racket or other sports equipment

When I was younger, I decided I wanted to play tennis professionally. I took tennis lessons, and I watched videos on how to play tennis. My parents even hired a coach to help me know how to play better. I practiced for hours, but no matter how hard I tried, I was never good enough to play professionally. So, I gave up professional tennis. Now, I just play for fun.

Imagine if I hired the most famous tennis player ever to teach me, someone like Serena Williams or Rodger Federer. Do you think I could become as good as that tennis player? I don't. I might get a little better, but I'd never be as good as them. But imagine if that tennis player could somehow get inside of me and play the game through me. If that were to happen, I could become a professional tennis player because I wouldn't be playing the game with my abilities. I'd have their abilities.

That's what the Holy Spirit does. He lives inside of you, and the more you cooperate with Him, the more He can operate through you. You don't have to do it alone or try with your own abilities. You have the Holy Spirit to help you, guide you, comfort you, and live the Christian life through you.

Response Time:

Pray a general pray and ask the Holy Spirit to help and guide the students. Then lead the students into seeking the Holy Spirit. Encourage students to be filled or refilled with the Holy Spirit. Play worship music, and lay hands on the students as you see God moving upon them. After worship, recap what God did for them.

Small Group Chat: Holy Spirit Helpers

Read 2 Corinthians 1:3-4 (ICB). *Praise be to the God and Father of our Lord Jesus Christ. God is the Father who is full of mercy. And he is the God of all comfort. He comforts us every time we have trouble, so that we can comfort others when they have trouble. We can comfort them with the same comfort that God gives us.*

Explain to the students that just as the Holy Spirit helps us and comforts us, He wants us to help others and comfort them. In a way, the Holy Spirit wants us to be His helpers.

Have the students make suggestions about how they can help the Holy Spirit by helping others. Encourage them to find someone to help this week. Have them ask the Holy Spirit to show them who they can help. Encourage them to write down what happened and share it next week during church.

Lesson 4: The Holy Spirit Reveals Things

Focus Point: The Holy Spirit reveals things to us.

Goal: Students will learn the Holy Spirit reveals things to them in a variety of ways.

Verse of the Day: Acts 2:17 (NIV) *"In the last days," God says, "I will pour out my Spirit on all people. Your sons and daughters will prophesy, your young men will see visions, your old men will dream dreams."*

Supplies Needed:

- doctor puppet or doctor costume for skit
- portable toolbox with various tools
- Tyler the Power Tool Guy Skit: Tyler wears a portable toolbox or toolbelt with various tools and is dressed in blue jeans and a plaid shirt, etc.
- optional: electric stud finder
- beanbag or ball
- sound effects of a storm (optional)
- radio
- Bible
- rubber or toy ear
- cross
- battery tester
- batteries

Opening: *Power Tools Countdown* (optional) or *Power Tools* Slide

Welcome: Holy Spirit Reveals Things

Welcome. During small group last week, you were all encouraged to find someone to help just as the Holy Spirit helps us. Did any of you do this? Allow students to tell their stories. *When you saw who needed your help, it was the Holy Spirit revealing these people to you. That's what we're going to talk about today. The Holy Spirit reveals things to us.*

Prayer: Have a student pray over the service.

Rules: (use rules slide) Go over the 5 Ups Rules.

Go over the *5 Ups Rules*: 1. Sit up straight. 2. Listen up. 3. Hush up. 4. Don't get up and run around or go to the bathroom. 5. Worship Up! (stand up and participate during praise and worship)

Theme or Activity Songs: Choose one of two fast moving activity or theme songs that go with the curriculum.

Game Time: I Spy (use game time slide)

Supplies needed: none

Play the I Spy game with your students. Choose an object you can see. Try to choose something hard to guess. Say, "I spy with my little eye something (choose a color). Students will take turns asking questions or making guesses until someone guesses correctly. The student who guesses gets to pick the object next.

When the game is over, tell your students that just as you gave hints such as the color to reveal the object, the Holy Spirit wants to reveal things to us.

Memory Verse Skit: (use Holy Spirit Power Lesson 4, slide A)

Supplies needed: doctor puppet or doctor costume for skit

Doctor Word: Hi kids. I'm Doctor Word. I'm called that because I'm a doctor and because I love the Word of God. You would think doctors know everything about medicine, but sometimes we have cases that stump us. One time, I had a patient that presented symptoms for Covid. I tested him three or four times, but he always tested negative. At first, I thought he might have a common flu virus, but his symptoms got worse. I tested for pneumonia and bronchitis, and I tried antibiotics. Nothing worked. I prayed and asked God what I should do. That night, I had a dream. During the dream, I saw the patient. He turned to me and said, "I have Respiratory System Virus." Then I woke up. I knew God gave me that dream to reveal what was wrong with my patient. RSV can be a serious illness for babies and older patients, but it's often mistaken for something else and has the same symptoms as Covid. When I knew what was wrong, I knew how to treat my patient. God reveals things to us in a variety of ways. Our verse for today is Acts 2:17 (NIV). *"In the last days," God says, "I will pour out my Spirit on all people. Your sons and daughters will prophesy, your young men will see visions, your old men will dream dreams."*

Offering: How Much Should I Give?

We should always give a tithe in the offering. A tithe is ten percent of whatever we make. So, if you get a ten-dollar allowance, you should give one dollar. Sometimes God will reveal to us that He wants us to give more that the ten percent. He gives us an impression of how much money we should give in the offering. When He does that, if we obey Him, He will bless us.

Skit: Tyler the Power Tool Guy's Revealing Power Tool

Supplies Needed: optional: electric stud finder. Tyler has a portable toolbox or toolbelt with various tools and is dressed in blue jeans and a plaid shirt, etc. If you use a girl in the skit, have her dress the same and call her Tyler the Power Tool Gal.

Tyler the Power Tool Guy: (Comes in) I hear that your teaching today about the Holy Spirit revealing things you can't see.

Leader:　　That's right, Tyler.

Tyler:　　That's great. Today, I want to tell you about a power tool that reveals things you can't see.

Leader:　　That's amazing. What power tool is that?

Tyler: (optional: shows stud finder) It's an electric stud finder.

Leader: An electric stud finder? What does that do?

Tyler: Part of the renovation involves hanging pictures. To do that, I need to find the studs or wood behind the walls. I could do that by knocking on the walls until I find the wood, but with a stud finder, I don't have to do that. I can use the stud finder to find the wood beams holding up the wall that I can't see.

Leader: That's amazing. So this stud find reveals things you can't see just like the Holy Spirit reveals things we don't know.

Tyler: That's right. I think I'm going to rename it. I'm going to call it my power wood revealer. I have to go now.

(Exits)

Verse of the Day: Acts 2:17 (NIV) *"In the last days," God says, "I will pour out my Spirit on all people. Your sons and daughters will prophesy, your young men will see visions, your old men will dream dreams."*

Memory Verse Talk: (use Holy Spirit Power Lesson 4, slide A)

Supplies needed: none

Acts 2:17 (NIV) says, "In the last days," God says, "I will pour out my Spirit on all people. Your sons and daughters will prophesy, your young men will see visions, your old men will dream dreams."

Because of this Scripture, we know the Holy Spirit sometimes reveals things to us in prophesy, visions, and dreams. Prophesy is when the Holy Spirit speaks through someone. Visions are when the Holy Spirit shows us things through pictures or images. Sometimes visions will be so real, it will be like we're watching something happen. Dreams are when the Holy Spirit shows us something in a dream, not just anytime we remember our dreams. We'll talk more about these later, but the important thing to remember is there's no age limit on this. If you are a Christian, God may choose to reveal things to you through any of these methods.

Memory Verse Activity: Memory Verse Hot Potato

Supplies needed: beanbag or ball

Rehearse the verse a few times. Have the students play a game of hot potato. They will arrange their chairs in a circle. Start the game by saying the verse address and passing the beanbag to one of the students. That student will say the first word in the verse when the beanbag and pass the beanbag to the next student who will say the second word of the verse. Continue passing the beanbag around the circle until the verse has been said several times. If it takes a student more than three seconds to say the next word, that student is out.

Bible Story: Prophecy, Dreams, and Visions

(Acts 27; Acts 16:1-10; Acts 22:6-10)

Supplies needed: sound effects of a storm (optional)

Sometimes even adults have a hard time understanding prophecy, dreams, and visions, so we're going to look at three stories in the book of Acts where God revealed things to the Apostle Paul using prophecy, dreams, visions, and other methods.

Turn on storm sound effects. *In Acts 27, Paul was aboard a ship as a prisoner headed to Rome. The weather started getting bad, and the sailing became dangerous. Paul felt an impression from the Holy Spirit and told the leaders on the ship to dock in Crete or the storm would become even more dangerous. God revealed this to Paul through a Word of Knowledge. A Word of Knowledge is when God reveals something to you that you wouldn't know otherwise.*

The leaders didn't listen, and the storm got worse. Things got so bad that everyone thought they were going to die. At this point, God gave Paul a vision and a prophetic word. This is what Paul heard and said in verses 23-26 (NIV). "Last night an angel of the God to whom I belong and whom I serve stood beside me and said, 'Do not be afraid, Paul. You must stand trial before Caesar; and God has graciously given you the lives of all who sail with you.' So keep up your courage, men, for I have faith in God that it will happen just as he told me. Nevertheless, we must run aground on some island."

This encouraged and comforted the men on the ship. Fourteen days later, they were saved when the ship ran aground on the island of Malta. God had saved everyone on the ship.

Another time, *in Acts 16, Paul and his companions were traveling the countryside telling people about Jesus. Every time they tried to go in a certain direction, the Holy Spirit impressed upon them not to go that way. Sometimes, the Holy Spirit will give us discernment, an uneasy feeling in our sprits, to show us we shouldn't go somewhere or do something. That's what happened to Paul. Finally, they stopped for the night and went to sleep. While they were sleeping, Paul had a dream. In his dream, he saw a man from Macedonia saying, "Come over here and help us." Paul knew the Holy Spirit gave him that dream because they were supposed to head in that direction. Sometimes God shows us things in our dreams. You'll know when you have a God dream because you'll remember the dream in detail, and you'll feel a stirring in your spirit. If you don't know what your God dream means, ask the Holy Spirit to reveal the meaning. If you still are unsure, ask an adult you trust to help you.*

Paul had many visions in his lifetime. I'm going to tell you what happened when he was given the first vision he ever had. It happened when Paul was younger. He hated Christians and was trying to kill them or arrest them. He was on the road to Damascus when he saw a vision.

In Acts 22:6-10 NIV, Paul told leaders in Jerusalem his vision. This is what he said. "About noon as I came near Damascus, suddenly a bright light from heaven flashed around me. I fell to the ground and heard a voice say to me, 'Saul! Saul! Why do you persecute me?'

"'Who are you, Lord?' I asked.

"'I am Jesus of Nazareth, whom you are persecuting,' he replied.

"My companions saw the light, but they did not understand the voice of him who was speaking to me.

"'What shall I do, Lord?' I asked.

" 'Get up,' the Lord said, 'and go into Damascus. There you will be told all that you have been

assigned to do.''

When Paul saw that vision, he gave his life to God.

Just as the Holy Spirit revealed things to Paul in prophecy, dreams, vision, words of knowledge, discernment, and impressions, the Holy Spirit will reveal things to you if you listen to Him, not with your ears but with your spirit.

Praise and Worship: Choose a couple of fast song and a slow song to lead children into praise and worship. It works well to talk to the children about what worship is and why it's important before you enter into this time. You can have a children's praise team, but until they understand leading praise and worship, have an adult leader or yourself be the worship leader.

Object Lessons:

5. Hearing God's Voice

Supplies needed: radio, Bible, rubber or toy ear (optional: show your own ear), cross

Show radio. *Do any of you have a radio? Most people have a radio in their car or on their alarm clocks, but people don't listen to the radio as much as they used to. When I was young (or my mom or grandma was young depending on your age), cell phones were something most kids didn't have, and even if they did, they couldn't listen to music on them. Most kids listened to CD players (cassette players, record players, eight-track players) or the radio when the wanted to listen to music.*

Turn on the radio. *Sometimes, if reception was bad, all you could get was static. You had to try to tune the radio in order to get the right station.* Tune the radio so it gets static, then tune it to a station.

Listening to the Holy Spirit when He reveals things is a lot like tuning a radio. Sometimes it's hard to understand what He is saying, but as we tune our spiritual ears and listen to His voice, we will get a clearer signal on what he is trying to say.

John 16:13-14 (NIV) gives a few guidelines for tuning into the Holy Spirit. "But when he, the Spirit of truth, comes, he will guide you into all the truth. He will not speak on his own; he will speak only what he hears, and he will tell you what is yet to come. He will glorify me because it is from me that he will receive what he will make known to you."

Show Bible. *The Holy Spirit guides us in truth. He will never tell us anything that goes against the Word of God.*

Show rubber or toy ear or point to your own ear. *The Holy Spirit only tells us what He hears from God the Father and God the Son. If you're hearing something that would cause you to sin or doubt God, you are tuning into the wrong channel.*

Show cross. *The Holy Spirit glorifies Jesus. Anything the Holy Spirit tells you will lift up and glorify Jesus in your life.*

Another way to know if you are hearing right is to pray. Ask God to give you wisdom and

discernment about what you're hearing. When you do this, if what you are hearing is of the Holy Spirit, you'll get a stronger signal. Tune radio to a strong signal. *If not, the signal will fade.* Tune radio to static.

Another way is to talk to a spiritual leader in your life. Suggest certain people you have talked to ahead of time. Choose leaders who understand God speaks to children.

6. Object Lesson: Prophetic Tester

Supplies needed: battery tester, batteries

Show battery tester. *This is a battery tester. When I want to know if a battery has a charge, I use it to test the battery.* Demonstrate the battery tester on the batteries and tell your students how much of a charge each battery has.

Did you know the Holy Spirit gives you a prophecy tester and wants you to use it? That tester is called discernment.

1 Thessalonians 5:20-21 says, "Do not treat prophecies with contempt but test them all; hold on to what is good,"

Here's how to use your discernment. Whenever there is a prophecy, vision, dream, or word of knowledge, whether it is given to you or if you are the one who receives the prophecy, ask God to help you use your discernment detector. Here's some questions you should ask:

Does it lift up Jesus?

Does it confirm what the Bible says?

Does it set well with what the Holy Spirit is telling you? Sometimes someone will try to give you a word that goes against what the Holy Spirit is telling you even though it doesn't go against Scripture. I'll give you an example. The Holy Spirit has led me to be a children's pastor. If someone prophecies that I should stop being a children's pastor and become a missionary in China, I will ask God if I'm wrong about what He is saying to me or if the prophecy is wrong? If God is telling me to be a children's pastor, the Holy Spirit won't tell someone to tell me to do something else instead. The Holy Spirit will speak to me first as long as I'm listening to Him and confirm what He's saying with a prophetic word.

There is one more discernment test. This is found in 1 Corinthians 14:3 (NKJ). "But he who prophesies speaks edification and exhortation and comfort to men."

Edification means to lift someone to become stronger spiritually. Things like you don't have what it takes to be a strong Christian would always be a false prophecy.

Exhortation means encouraging someone to grow closer to God. That means somebody isn't going to prophecy that I should worship or read my Bible so much.

Comfort means to comfort or encourage someone. If a prophecy tears you down or discourages you, it is a false prophecy.

What happens if someone gives a prophecy that you detect isn't from the Holy Spirit. Always operate in love. Love is more important in the Kingdom of God than prophecy. First, pray for the person. Second, talk to an adult you trust. Recommend leaders you've talked to ahead of time. Third, declare that you don't receive that prophecy, but most of the time, you don't want to say it out loud in front of the person. You may want to get alone to say this or say it in a quiet voice only God can hear.

As you operate in the prophetic more, it will be easier to know what is the Holy Spirit and what isn't. Trust the Holy Spirit to lead you, and talk to adults you trust.

Message: Listening to the Holy Spirit

Preparation: This message asks you to talk about times the Holy Spirit has revealed things in your life. If you have areas where you don't have experience, ask adults in your congregation to give testimonies and examples for these things. If you can, choose leaders that you approve to guide students in the prophetic.

The Holy Spirit wants to reveal things to you. He does this in a variety of ways.

The most important way the Holy Spirit reveals things to us is through the Word of God. The more we learn the Word of God, the more the Holy Spirit will show us what it means and how to apply it to our lives. Tell about a time God has done this in your life.

Another way the Holy Spirit reveals things is to impress things on us in our spirits. Tell about a time God has done this in your life.

The Holy Spirit gives us Words of Wisdom and Words of Knowledge. This is when we know something or we know what to do about something even though there's no way we could know if the Holy Spirit didn't show us. Tell about a time God has done this in your life.

The Holy Spirit gives us dreams. We sometimes have dreams that are just dreams, but sometimes the Holy Spirit will show us things in our dreams. Tell about a time God has done this in your life.

The Holy Spirit gives us visions. Visions sometimes are pictures that come to our mind that we know the Holy Spirit shows us. Sometimes visions are just an impression of an image, and sometimes visions are so strong we can feel like we are really seeing something or experiencing something. This is called an open vision. Tell about a time God has done this in your life.

The Holy Spirit gives us prophetic messages to speak to people. Sometimes, these messages are an image or just a few words. Other times, the Holy Spirit gives us entire sentences to speak or a Scripture. Tell about a time God has done this in your life.

The Holy Spirit revelations are not always easy to interpret or tune in, but as we learn to listen to the Holy Spirit, it's easier to operate in the prophetic. Ask an adult you trust to help you connect what you're hearing to Scripture and to know if you are hearing right, and don't be afraid of making a mistake. That's the only way to learn.

Response Time:

Preparation: Ask the adult leaders you've chosen from your congregation who are spiritual to help you with this.

Explain to your students that we are going to pray for the Holy Spirit. to use us prophetically. Have students who have been baptized in the Holy Spirit pray in tongues. Have the other students pray and worship in their native language.

After praying for a while, ask your adult volunteers to sit in chairs in front. Ask your students if any of them have a word or an image to speak to any of the adults. Encourage them if they're timid at first. You may have to give an example by having an adult give a word. As the students do this, allow the Holy Spirit to lead you as you interpret these words according to Scripture. If an adult volunteer wants to add information to any of the words spoken, encourage them to do so. This will encourage students to speak when they have a word in a safe way and place without worrying about harsh judgement.

At the end, encourage students to go to you, their parents, or one of these volunteers when they have a message from the Holy Spirit. In this way, they will grow in the prophetic while learning to hear the Holy Spirit more effectively.

Small Group Chat: Picture This

Supplies needed: paper, colored pencils or markers

Have the students draw pictures of things the Holy Spirit is showing them. Allow them to show these pictures and talk about them.

Encourage the students to have a notebook with them at all times, even at night, so they can write or draw what the Holy Spirit is showing them.

Lesson 5: The Holy Spirit Gives Us His Power

Focus Point: The Holy Spirit works through us with His power.

Goal: Students will learn they can heal and perform miracles when they do so with the power of the Holy Spirit.

Verse of the Day: Zechariah 4:6b (NIV) *"Not by might nor by power, but by my Spirit," says the Lord Almighty.*

Supplies Needed:

- doctor puppet or doctor costume for skit
- portable toolbox with various tools
- Tyler the Power Tool Guy Skit: Tyler wears a portable toolbox or toolbelt with various tools and is dressed in blue jeans and a plaid shirt, etc.
- small power tool
- a balloon for each student
- duct tape or string
- basketball
- ping pong ball
- hair dryer
- 2 name tags
- marker
- olive oil or essential oil

Opening: *Power Tools Countdown* (optional) or *Power Tools* Slide

Welcome: Holy Spirit Power

Welcome. For the last four weeks, we've been learning about Holy Spirit Power. We've learned we can receive power through the baptism of the Holy Spirit. We've learned the Holy Spirit gives us boldness, helps us, and reveals things to us. Today, we are going to learn more about the power of the Holy Spirit and how He can do miraculous things through us.

Prayer: Have a student pray over the service.

Rules: (use rules slide) Go over the 5 Ups Rules.

Go over the *5 Ups Rules*: 1. Sit up straight. 2. Listen up. 3. Hush up. 4. Don't get up and run around or go to the bathroom. 5. Worship Up! (stand up and participate during praise and worship)

Theme or Activity Songs: Choose one of two fast moving activity or theme songs that go with the curriculum.

Game Time: A Mighty Rushing Balloon (use game time slide)

Supplies needed: a balloon for each student, duct tape or string

Preparation: Make a large circle with duct tape or string.

You might want to ask your students questions about the previous Holy Spirit Power lessons to decide who participates, or if you have a smaller group, everyone could participate.

Explain to the students how the game is played. Each student playing will receive a deflated balloon. They will stand back to back in the center of the duct tape circle. When the leader says go, each one will blow up his balloon and let go of it allowing it to deflate. The student will then stand where his balloon landed. The first student to escape the circle wins.

It was almost impossible to get the balloon to go where you want it no matter how hard you try. We can't control the Holy Spirit by using our power or might. We can only cooperate with the Holy Spirit. When He moves, we move with Him.

Memory Verse Skit: (use Holy Spirit Power Lesson 4, slide A)

Supplies needed: doctor puppet or doctor costume for skit

Doctor Word: Hi kids. I'm Doctor Word. I'm called that because I'm a doctor and because I love the Word of God. One of the hardest things to get used to as a doctor is that I can't cure everyone. No matter how hard I try or how much I learn, I don't have the power to heal people. Only the Holy Spirit has that power. That's why today's memory verse is so important to me. Zechariah 4:6b (NIV) says, *"'Not by might nor by power, but by my Spirit,' says the Lord Almighty."* The Holy Spirit is the one who has the power to miraculously heal and do miracles.

Offering: Multiplication

Did you know that when you give in the offering, God has the power to multiply your offering? That's right. I know this because in John 6, the disciples told Jesus that they didn't have enough food to feed the multitudes that had come to hear Jesus speak. A boy offered his lunch, but it was only five small loaves of bread and two small fish. Jesus blessed it and had the disciples pass out the food. Jesus multiplied the boy's offering. It not only fed all 5,000 people, but there were twelve large baskets of food left over.

Skit: Tyler the Power Tool Guy Greatest Job

Supplies Needed: small power tool, Tyler has a portable toolbox or toolbelt with various tools and is dressed in blue jeans and a plaid shirt, etc. If you use a girl in the skit, have her dress the same and call her Tyler the Power Tool Gal.

Tyler the Power Tool Guy: (Comes in carrying a small power tool) This is my favorite job ever.

Leader: Hi, Tyler. Are you still renovating that old house?

Tyler: I sure am. It's been a lot of fun.

Leader: What makes this job better than you're other jobs?

Tyler: (shows power tool) Are you kidding me? I get to use so many of my power tools.

Leader: That's awesome. I know you love your power tools. Which power tools have you used so far?

Tyler: I do love my power tools. I got to use a chainsaw and jackhammer for cutting out walls, floors, and cabinets. I got to use my jigsaw for cutting out door and window frames and my circular saw for cutting wood planks for beams and fireplace mantles. I used my drill for screws and my nail gun for nails. I used other power tools too, but there isn't enough time to mention them all. Ahh. God is good to me.

Leader: I'm so happy for you. When will the job be finished?

Tyler: I started five weeks ago. I should be done in another week or two.

Leader: That's fast for everything you had to do.

Tyler: Not really. That's fairly typical.

Leader: I'm curious. In the past, people didn't have power tools. How did they renovate or build houses then.

Tyler: You mean in the dark ages?

Leader: Not exactly the dark ages but many years ago.

Tyler: I consider it the dark ages because these people didn't have power tools to make things easier. They had to use manual tools. It was a lot harder work, and it took much longer to do anything.

Leader: So, they used power, but it was their own power not electric power.

Tyler: That's right.

Leader: That reminds me of today's lesson. When we use our own might or power, we can't do much, but the power of the Holy Spirit changes everything.

Tyler: I never thought about it that way, but you're right. I have to go now. I have more work to do, and today I get to use this tool. (Shows tool and tells what it does.)

(Exits)

Verse of the Day: Zechariah 4:6b (NIV) *"Not by might nor by power, but by my Spirit," says the Lord Almighty.*

Memory Verse Talk: (use Holy Spirit Power Lesson 5, slide A)

Supplies needed: basketball

Zechariah 4:6b (NIV) says, " 'Not by might nor by power, but by my Spirit, '" says the Lord Almighty.

What that means is there is no way we can do anything for God that makes any difference when we try to do it on our own. The only way we can make a difference for God is if we allow the Holy Spirit to do things through us.

Remember a couple of weeks ago, when I taught the lesson about how the Holy Spirit is like a coach who plays the game through us?

Start bouncing the basketball. *If I decided I wanted to be a famous basketball player like Michael Jordon or Labron James, I could practice for years and not be as good as them. I don't have the skill or experience they do. But if I could get Labron James to step inside of me and play basketball through me, then I'd be as good a basketball player as he is.*

I can't live a Christian life or get someone saved or healed on my own. I don't have enough power or might to do anything like that on my own. But I have the Holy Spirit living inside of me. It's through His power and might that I can do miraculous things for the Kingdom of God.

Memory Verse Activity: Bouncing Verse

Supplies needed: basketball

Have the students stand in a circle. For larger groups, you can have more than one circle. Have them bounce the ball to each other. Whenever a student gets the ball, he or she has to say the next word in the memory verse and bounce the ball to another student. Do this until the verse has been said several times.

Bible Story: Walking and Leaping and Praising God

(Acts 3:1-16)

Supplies needed: none

Instruct the students to do the following, or choose a few students to stand in front and do the motions for the other students. When you say walking or walk, they are to walk two steps. When you say leaping or leap, they are to jump up and down two times. When you say praising God or praise God, they are to throw their hands in the air and shout praise the Lord. Have them practice a few times.

One day, Peter and John went to the temple to pray. In front of the gate was a man who had been lame all of his life. He didn't have anyone to provide for him, so he sat in front of the gate everyday and asked for money.

*Peter told the man to look at them. The man did because he thought they were going to give him some money. Instead, Peter said, "I don't have any money, but what I do have, I'm going to give to you. In the name of Jesus, rise up and **walk**."*

The man must have been confused. Peter and John didn't have the power or might to heal him. He'd probably been to several doctors, and none of them could heal him. And these men weren't doctors. What the man didn't know was Peter and John had the Holy Spirit living inside of them. Through the Holy Spirit and in the Name of Jesus, they did have the power to heal him.

Peter and John took the man's hand and pulled him to his feet. Instantly, the man was healed. He went ***walking***, *and* ***leaping***, *and* ***praising God*** *into the temple courts. Everyone was amazed to see him up* *and **walking** around and **leaping** in the air.*

The people in the temple were so amazed, they surrounded Peter and John. Peter told them it wasn't by his power that He healed the man. It was by the power of the Holy Spirit and in the name of Jesus that the man was healed.

*We don't know what eventually happened to the man, but he's probably **walking**, and **leaping**, and **praising** God in Heaven right now thanks to the power of the Holy Spirit.*

Optional Song: Walking and Leaping Song

If your students enjoy being silly, have them sing the Walking and Leaping Song with motions in a silly way. Here is a link to the song on YouTube. https://youtu.be/ymUnSwFyFzM

Praise and Worship: Choose a couple of fast song and a slow song to lead children into praise and worship. It works well to talk to the children about what worship is and why it's important before you enter into this time. You can have a children's praise team, but until they understand leading praise and worship, have an adult leader or yourself be the worship leader.

Object Lessons:

1. Floating Ping Pong Balls

Supplies needed: ping pong ball, hair dryer

Show ping pong ball. *I have here a ping pong ball. This ping pong ball represents us. This ping pong ball want to float in the air, but it can't.* Demonstrate by holding the ball in the air several times and letting it drop. You could also have the students try to get it to float.

This ping pong ball doesn't have the strength or power to float in the air on its own. It needs help.

Show hair dryer. *This hair dryer represents the Holy Spirit.*

Point the nozzle of the hair dryer up. Place the ping pong ball on the nozzle of the hair dryer, and turn the hair dryer on. The air from the hair dryer should keep the ping pong ball in the air.

The ping pong ball needs the power of the hair dryer to make it float just as we need the power of the Holy Spirit.

2. The Name of Jesus (Use Holy Spirit Power Lesson 5, slide B)

Supplies needed: 2 name tags, marker

Preparation: Using a marker, write your name on one name tag. Write Jesus Christ on the other name tag.

The Holy Spirit wants to operate through you to heal people and do miracles, but you can't do it in your own power. You can pray for someone to be healed by your own power and name and nothing will happen. Place your name badge on your shirt. *If I tried to heal someone using my own name and power, I might as well save my breath. I don't have the might or power to do miracles.*

119

Place Jesus Christ name badge over your name badge. *When the Holy Spirit works through me in the name of Jesus Christ, it is different.*

Show slide B. Mark 16:17-18 (NIV) says, *"And these signs will accompany those who believe: In my name they will drive out demons; they will speak in new tongues; they will pick up snakes with their hands; and when they drink deadly poison, it will not hurt them at all; they will place their hands on sick people, and they will get well."*

When the Holy Spirit works through me in the name of Jesus Christ, then I have Holy Spirit power to drive out demons in the name of Jesus Christ. I can speak in tongues in the name of Jesus Christ. If I encounter a snake or poison, the Holy Spirit gives me the power to declare it won't hurt me in the name of Jesus Christ. And if I lay my hands on sick people in the name of Jesus Christ and tell them to be healed, they will get well.

I can do nothing on my own, but in the name of Jesus Christ, through the power of the Holy Spirit, I can do the miraculous.

So, what happens if it doesn't work. That's not on me. It is the name of Jesus Christ through the power of the Holy Spirit. It is not me. God wants me to speak in the name of Jesus Christ. It's up to Him what happens next. I don't have the power to make anything happen on my own.

Optional Object Lesson: The Oil (Use Holy Spirit Power Lesson 5, slide C)

Supplies needed: Olive oil or essential oil

Mark 6:13 talks about the disciples. It says, "And they were casting out many demons and were anointing with oil many sick people and healing them."

Have you ever seen someone prayed for when the pastor or whoever is praying anoints that person with oil? Allow students to answer. Usually, the person praying will place a little olive oil and essential oil on someone's forehead and then place their hand gently on the person head. If the person praying is praying for something specific, he will usually make his request. If not, he might say something like, "More Lord," or "Touch them, Lord."

There is no power in the oil, but the oil is a symbol of the Holy Spirit. It's a way of saying the Holy Spirit is doing the work, not us.

I'm going to demonstrate to show you how this works. Ask for a volunteer. Ask God to move on the student you choose. Make sure to have a catcher behind the student. Place a dab of oil on your finger and place it on the student's forehead. Place your hand gently on the person's head. Pray in tongues or say something like, "In the Name of Jesus," or "More, Lord." Wait, and leave your hand on the student's head. Don't try to make something happen. This is up to the Holy Spirit. Wait on Him. If God moves, talk about what happened. If He doesn't, go on without comment.

I just demonstrated how you can pray for someone else using anointing oil. If you don't have oil, don't worry about it. There's nothing special about the oil. We use it because Scripture tells up it represents the Holy Spirit.

Did you know that you can pray for yourself by laying hands on your head and anointing yourself with oil?

You can anoint your head with oil before you go to bed and ask the Holy Spirit for dreams and visions. You can anoint your eyelids and ask the Holy Spirit to help you see in the spirit. You can anoint your palms with oil and ask the Holy Spirit to heal you or to use you when you pray for others to be healed. You can even anoint your room at home or your locker or desk at school and ask God to get rid of anything evil in your home or school and fill it with the Holy Spirit.

As I said before, there is nothing magical in the oil. By using oil, you are showing that you're not relying on your own power but on the power of the Holy Spirit.

Message: Power to Heal

Supplies needed: olive oil or essential oil

Preparation: Before this week's lesson, ask someone who was healed to give a testimony in Children's Church. If you have a healing testimony, you can choose yourself for this. Also let the congregation know that you are going to have your students pray for the sick. If anyone is sick and needs prayer, they should come to this week's children's church. You may need to ask your pastor to announce this, or you can go to individual people who need prayer.

Show slide B. Mark 16:17-18 (NIV) says, *"And these signs will accompany those who believe: In my name they will drive out demons; they will speak in new tongues; they will pick up snakes with their hands; and when they drink deadly poison, it will not hurt them at all; they will place their hands on sick people, and they will get well."*

It doesn't say anything about an age limit here. Any believer in Christ has the power to heal, not because of his own power, but because the Holy Spirit lives inside of him.

Have someone give a testimony of being healed.

Response Time: Healing Altar Ministry

For this time, make sure you have catchers and prayer warriors to assist you.

Invite anyone who needs healed, delivered, or needs the baptism of the Holy Spirit to come forward. Ask adults to sit in chairs so students can touch their heads when they pray for them. Also ask students who need healed or the baptism of the Holy Spirit to come forward. Ask those who need healed or delivered to stand on the right side and those who need the baptism of the Holy Spirit to stand on the left.

If you have never done anything like this before, remember this is not in your own power. Trust the Holy Spirit to show up and work the miraculous. It's not up to you. It's up to Him.

Before we do anything, we're going to spend some time worshipping. If you are baptized in the Holy Spirit worship and pray in tongues.

After a time of prayer and worship, instruct the students. *First, come and place a dab of oil on your finger. You're going to pray for these people to be healed and deliver or baptized in the Holy Spirit.*

Instruct your students to place the oil on the person's forehead, then place their hands on the person's head. If there is more than one student praying for each person, instruct them to place hands on the center of their backs. Have them command what they are praying for. For instance, "Be healed," or "Be delivered," or "Be filled." Then have the students pray these simple prayers, worship, or speak in tongues. Students can also be silent. Go through the prayer line. Give instruction when needed. Touch the students backs as they pray to add your faith and anointing to theirs.

When the prayer time is over, ask for testimonies of people who were healed, delivered, and baptized in the Holy Spirit.

Small Group Chat: Prayer Clothes

Supplies needed: square pieces of cloth or handkerchiefs, olive oil or essential oil

Do you know people who are sick and can't get to church or don't want to go to church to be prayed for? Sometimes you can pray for them at their homes, but sometimes you can pray over a piece of cloth and give them that cloth. The Holy Spirit can use those cloths to heal people.

Acts 19:11-12 (NIV) says, God did extraordinary miracles through Paul, so that even handkerchiefs and aprons that had touched him were taken to the sick, and their illnesses were cured and the evil spirits left them.

We are going to take these cloths, anoint them with oil, and pray over them. I want you each to take at least one of them home and ask God who to give the cloth to. Let that person know you prayed over the cloth.

You might want to plan a field trip for your students to a hospital or nursing home to pass out these prayer clothes and pray for the patients.

About the Author

Pastor Tamera Kraft has been a children's pastor for over thirty years. She is the director of a ministry called Revival Fire For Kids where she mentors other children's leaders, teaches workshops, and is a children's ministry consultant and children's revivalist. She is a recipient of the 2007 National Children's Leaders Association Shepherd's Cup for lifetime achievement in children's ministry.

You can find out more about Revival Fire for Kids at http://revivalfire4kids.net.